SO YOU THINK YOU KNOW ABOUT FOOTBALL?

See if you can score with the Amazin' Mazer*

What was the most one-sided game in NFL history?

Who was the defensive end who ran 66 yards *the wrong way* for a touchdown, giving the opposition the score. . . ?

What was the most brutal game in the history of pro football?

Who was the first coach to win 100 games in a decade?

How did the players—and the teams—get their nicknames?

Who was the only man to run over 3000 yards in one season?

Which president of the US saved football from being labelled a "criminal sport. . . ?"

*It's in the book . . . and that's no joke!

Also by Bill Mazer

The Amazin' Bill Mazer's
Baseball Trivia Book

Published by
WARNER BOOKS

THE AMAZIN' BILL MAZER'S FOOTBALL TRIVIA BOOK

by Bill Mazer and
Stan Fischler

WARNER BOOKS

A Warner Communications Company

WARNER BOOKS EDITION

Copyright © 1981 by Stan Fischler and Dutch Enterprises, Inc.
All rights reserved.

Cover design by New Studio, Inc.

Cover photo by Tony Ruta

Warner Books, Inc., 75 Rockefeller Plaza, New York, N.Y. 10019

 A Warner Communications Company

Printed in the United States of America

First Printing: October, 1981

10 9 8 7 6 5 4 3 2 1

The authors wish to thank the following people, without whom this book could not have been written: George Hall, who was of extraordinary assistance in research and qualifies for an "Amazin' Mazer" bumper sticker, at the very least; not to mention Richard Friedman, Lori Weisman, Michael Fleming, Stewart Scharf, David Borsack, Matt Scheckner, Mike Barnes, Jory Levinton, Matthew Ryan, Larry Keller, Rick Miller, Ben Olan, Chris Pellettieri, Evan Charkes, Dave Lippman, Paul Ringe, Herman Zuker, and Paul Fichtenbaum, each of whom contributed ideas and assistance in one way or another. And special thanks to research editors Joe Carbone and Gabe Miller.

THE AMAZIN' BILL MAZER'S FOOTBALL TRIVIA BOOK

**Who was the first pro football player
to use an agent?**

Harold "Red" Grange. In his book *Hit the
Sign and Win a Free Suit of Clothes from Harry
Finklestein*, Bert Randolph Sugar described how
the relationship between Grange and the agent
Charles C. "C. C." Pyle was formed:

> On the night of October 25, 1925, a group
> of University of Illinois football players were
> taking in Rudolph Valentino's latest potboiler,
> *The Eagle*, at the Virginia Theatre in Cham-
> paign, Illinois. An usher came down the aisle
> and paused at the row where the football
> players were seated. Finding who he was
> looking for, he said, "Mr. Grange, Mr. Pyle
> would like to see you in his office."

The "Mr. Grange" in this scenario was, of course, Red Grange, the famed Illini football star. The "Mr. Pyle" was the owner of the Virginia Theatre, one of a string of movie houses he owned throughout Illinois and Indiana. Pyle had always provided team members with free tickets to his theaters, but neither Grange nor any of the other members of the team ever paid "any attention who they [the tickets] came from." Until that day at the Virginia Theatre, they neither knew Pyle nor had ever heard of him.

Grange followed the usher up the aisle and through the baroque lobby into the front office. Seated behind a desk was a florid man with a smartly trimmed mustache and graying hair, a fashion blueplate with two side dishes, spats, and a walking cane—the "best dressed man I ever met in my life," remembers Grange. He introduced himself as Charles Pyle and without any overture immediately got to the point: "Red, how would you like to make a million dollars?"

More than somewhat taken aback, Grange could only say, half in jest and half in surprise, "I don't do those things. I can't kill anybody."

The dapper theater owner went on, "No, I have in mind your becoming professional. I think we can set it up. I'll go to Chicago and talk to George Halas and the Bears and we'll set up a tour around the U.S." To emphasize his point, he added, "I think we'll do right well."

Pyle and Grange entered into an agreement that called for Pyle to receive one-third of the money Grange would earn playing football, appearing in motion pictures, and "other ventures."

A month later Grange signed a Pyle-negotiated contract with the Bears. The seeds had been planted. When sown they would reap headaches for countless owners and general managers during the 1950s, 60s, 70s, and 80s, when player-agent relationships became the rule rather than the exception.

**Name the opposing quarterbacks
in the only game, pro or college, in which
each threw six touchdown passes?**

On November 2, 1969, the St. Louis Cardinals faced the New Orleans Saints in one of the most exciting offensive games ever played. Charlie Johnson of the Cardinals and Billy Kilmer of the Saints each targeted six pigskin passes that resulted in touchdowns. The Saints won the battle in the end, 51–42.

**How do pro football teams come up
with their nicknames?**

Nicknames generally symbolize power and speed (Jets, Lions, Rams), predators (Falcons, Eagles, Bears), aggression (Raiders, Vikings, Giants), or the city in which the teams play (49ers, Oilers, Patriots). Nicknames give teams identi-

11

fication, imply majesty, and, of course, enable sportswriters to play verbal games.

Contests produced the names of many National Football League teams, particularly newer ones such as the Kansas City Chiefs, New England Patriots, Minnesota Vikings, and Oakland Raiders. Occasionally, contest winners backed their whims with reason. New Orleans takes its nickname from one of part-owner Al Hirt's favorite tunes, "When the Saints Go Marching In." Sentimentality ruled in Buffalo and Cincinnati, where the names of defunct teams were resurrected. In Buffalo in the late 1940s, there were three professional teams called the Bisons. When the confusion became too great, the pro football team, a member of the old All-America Football Conference, switched to the "Bills." Denver, on the other hand, had never had a pro football franchise and wanted to signal its arrival with a nickname that wasn't familiar: ergo, the Broncos. In Houston, the answer was simpler: owner Bud Adams was in the oil business.

Then we have the St. Louis (née Chicago) Cardinals, named not for the bird but for the color of some old faded jerseys belonging to the University of Chicago Maroons that former owner Chris O'Brien bestowed upon his pros. Up until then the Cardinals had been known, curiously enough, as the Chicago Normals because they played in Normal Field.

Some claim the San Diego (Née Los Angeles) Chargers were named by their original owner, Barron Hilton, when that hotel mogul was contemplating entering the charge-card business. Actually, the name is derived from the University of Southern California battle cry, "Charge!," which was popular in the Los Angeles Coliseum, the Chargers' first home.

In New York, the "Jets" presumably signify the planes flying in and out of nearby Kennedy and LaGuardia airports, although one suspects the mind of a poet lurked here, what with the baseball Mets already occupying Shea Stadium.

The reasoning behind team nicknames is not always as simple as one might think. When Bert Bell moved the Frankford (Pa.) Yellowjackets to Philadelphia, the eagle was more than a symbol of speed and strength. Those were the days when the country was trying to dig out of the Great Depression and the National Recovery Act (NRA) eagle was the symbol of President Franklin D. Roosevelt's New Deal. Bell saw a connection between his own new deal in bringing a franchise to Philadelphia and the patriotic history of the City of Brotherly Love, so he called his team the Eagles. The Cleveland Browns, on the other hand, simply adopted the name of their first coach and team architect, Paul Brown.

A university was behind the nickname given the Los Angeles Rams when they were originally located in Cleveland. The old Cleveland Rams took their name from their general manager's favorite college team, the Fordham Rams.

In some cities, the football team took its

name from an older baseball franchise. New York's first football team shared a stadium with the baseball Giants and therefore became the football Giants.

When did a referee show leniency to a losing coach?

In 1968, Joe Kurharich of the Philadelphia Eagles lost his first 11 games, then ended the season with a record of 2–12. Kurharich's miserable season was symbolized by one episode.

The winless Eagles were playing worse than usual one day and coach Kurharich had seen enough. He started yelling at his players from the sidelines. At last the referee warned him to stop coaching from the sidelines or be penalized five yards. At this point Kurharich yelled, "Hah! Shows you how much you know, that should have been a fifteen-yard penalty."

The referee turned and snapped, "That's okay, the way you're coaching this year, five yards is plenty!"

**When did a football coach, after seeing
his televised interview, threaten to sue
a pair of television sportscasters?**

During the winter of 1972 the New York
Giants were completing yet another in a long
line of awful seasons when Sal Marchiano, a
reporter for ABC-TV, taped an interview with
Giants coach Alex "Big Red" Webster.

Although Webster said little of consequence
to Marchiano, the recorded material nevertheless
was delivered to the ABC studios, where Marchiano's colleague, Jim Bouton, evaluated it. After
concluding that Webster's interview was virtually worthless as recorded, Bouton, being a crea-
tive type, elected to have some fun. Instead of
running the interview straight, Bouton decided
to run it backward, giving the effect of Webster
talking gibberish. But as luck would have it, the
sound never came off when the film was finally
shown on television, and all that emerged was
Webster doing a "silent" film.

Many viewers believed that it was a put-on—
which it was—and had a good laugh. But neither
Webster nor Giants boss Wellington Mara de-
rived any humor from the episode. Webster and
Mara huddled and decided that Bouton and
Marchiano should get their collective come-
uppance, and as a result they sued Bouton and
Marchiano.

A number of Grade-A movies about football have been turned out by Hollywood over the years. Can you name any of the films or the stars involved in them?

One of the earliest—and funniest—was *Horse Feathers* (1932) starring the four Marx Brothers (Groucho, Chico, Harpo, and Zeppo). In the flick Groucho, as president of Huxley College, recruited Harpo and Chico simply because they could play football—or so he thought. (Actually, Harpo was a dog catcher and Chico an inveterate opportunist.) The football match against Darwin College is the climax of the film, and Harpo's inventiveness saves the day for Huxley. He attaches elastic to the pigskin and spreads banana skins behind him on a long run, then with his brothers, leaps into his dog-catching "chariot" to chase a loose dog into the end zone; there he unloads a bunch of footballs, rocketing Huxley's point total to victory with each ball.

Hold That Co-Ed (1938) featured John Barrymore, the incomparable thespian, in a musical comedy co-starring George Murphy (later a California senator) and Joan Davis. The highlight of the film occurs when wacky Joan Davis enters the climactic football game during a tornado and her side-splitting efforts to crossbuck the winds results in a "Wrong Way" Roy Riegels run that wins the game.

President Ronald Reagan, Wayne Morris, and Eddie Albert starred in *Brother Rat* (1938), playing Virginia Military Institute football players who have girls—Priscilla Lane, Jane Bryan, and Jane Wyman, respectively—rather than studies on their minds. Their romantic antics nearly cost them gridiron glory.

Navy Blue and Gold (1940) gives us James Stewart, on his charming way to stardom, vying with Robert Young for the hand of Florence Rice (who in real life was the daughter of ace sportswriter Grantland Rice). Stretching the rules in the pursuit of romance nearly results in grid disaster for the Midshipmen, but a compassionate Lionel Barrymore saves the day for dear old Annapolis.

Perhaps the most famous role enacted by Ronald Reagan took place in *Knute Rockne, All-American* (1940). Reagan portrays George Gipp, the great young runner of Notre Dame. The movie, however, centers around Rockne, the legendary player and coach of the Fighting Irish. It was fitting, in a Hollywood kind of way, that a motion picture about one of football's great innovators and inspirational leaders should lead the way for future gridiron epics. It contains one of the screen's best-remembered moments: Pat O'Brien imploring his charges to go out and overcome Army's first-half lead and "win one for the Gipper." That one scene alone was so moving that it was responsible for the conversion of young boys from coast to coast, of every faith, far from the heartland of Indiana, into fans of the Fighting Irish.

Good News (1947), one of the liveliest musicals to come out of the MGM studio, is a story about a gridiron hero thrown for a loss by classes and lasses. Peter Lawford and June Allyson are the stars, singing such tunes as "Good News," "Lucky in Love," and "The French Lesson." Mel "The Velvet Fog" Torme comes through with a superb rendition of "The Best Things in Life Are Free."

Hollywood couldn't possibly miss out on a film about the incomparable Jim Thorpe and finally produced *Jim Thorpe, All-American* (1951). The compelling biography of the athlete who rose from obscure beginnings on an American Indian reservation to international fame pays considerable tribute to his prodigious gridiron prowess. It is an inspiring yet tragic record of one of America's sports greats. Burt Lancaster plays Thorpe, with support from Phyllis Thaxter as his wife.

Crazy Legs: All-American (1953) is the biography of Elroy Hirsch, star pass-catching end for the Chicago Rockets of the old All-America Football Conference and for the Los Angeles Rams. What surprised critics was the emergence of Crazy Legs himself as an actor of merit. Lloyd Nolan plays Hirsch's gruff high school coach and Joan Vohs plays his wife. This is an ingratiating story of a man born to humble circumstances who serves his country during World War II and returns to gridiron stardom only to be struck in the head, causing a loss of the coordination so crucial to an athlete. The happy ending is a true one: Crazy Legs overcomes the handicap and plays on the National Football League champions of 1951.

The truth-is-stranger-than-fiction journalism exploits of George Plimpton reached the screen with *Paper Lion* (1968). Here Plimpton weathers training camp with the Detroit Lions, passing himself off as a Harvard quarterback while allegedly trying out for an NFL job.

The Longest Yard (1974) is a prison melodrama with gridiron hijinx. Burt Reynolds plays an obnoxiously disrespectful hardhead who captains the Mean Machine, the State Prison football team. The story pivots around the unnatural lust of the villainous warden (Eddie Albert) for the Prison League championship. Other lust lies in wait in the warden's office in the person of Bernadette Peters, and the film cashes in on the popularity of former pro players Mike Henry, Pervis Atkins, Ray Nitschke, Ernie Wheelwright, Joe Kapp, and others who heave and spew against each other in the cells and on the field.

One of the best of all football movies is *Heaven Can Wait* (1978), concerning a Los Angeles Ram quarterback (Warren Beatty, who also coproduced and codirected the film). Quarterback Beatty is prematurely summoned to heaven by an overzealous celestial escort, Buck Henry. A sympathetic archangel (James Mason) returns Beatty to earth in the body of a business tycoon, but the only way he can rejoin the Rams is to buy the team. While getting his body back into shape, he is forced to escape attempts on his new life by the tycoon's unfaithful wife (Dyan Cannon) and treacherous male secretary (Charles Grodin). Meanwhile he falls in love with an English woman (Julie Christie) leading a protest against the possible destruction of her village by one of his corporations. Just prior to the Super Bowl, a murder attempt finally is successful. But there is a divine game plan, after all.

Beatty is granted a substitute body from the untimely death of his backup quarterback and he leads the Rams to the championship. However, he's been warned by Mason that he will recall none of the events—even his lady love —of the previous few months. Beatty runs into Christie after the game and although they don't recognize each other, they have that feeling they've met before.

Football movies came into their own during the boom of the pro leagues in the late 1960s, when public interest swung sharply to the violence of contact sports. Television proved to be the medium that sparked football mania. Coincidentally, the techniques of TV coverage enhanced the impact of gridiron action on the motion-picture screen. Among the hard-hitting football films of the 1970s were *Semi-Tough*, *The Longest Yard*, and *North Dallas Forty*.

The score 73–0 has enormous significance in National Football League annals. Why?

It represents the most one-sided result of any NFL championship game. The "73" belonged to the Chicago Bears; the "0" to the Washington Redskins.

This slaughter on the gridiron took place on a weather-perfect afternoon on December 8, 1940, at Washington's Griffith Stadium. There were 36,034 fans in the stands expecting the hometown Redskins to give the visiting Bears what-for and take the professional football title.

And why not? Just three weeks earlier the Redskins had beaten the Bears, 7–3, and there seemed little different about the two teams now. But the difference became apparent within a minute of the opening kickoff.

Shortly after the 50-second mark the Bears had passed for a touchdown. It was the first of three Chicago touchdowns in the first period. They were to register one in the second, four in the third, and three in the last. In no aspect of the game did the Bears fail to execute to perfection. Their ground game pierced the Redskin defense with impunity. They connected at will on the passes, although the air attack was less frequently employed, and their defense hermetically sealed the foe.

Chicago coach George Halas did not rely on his starting varsity to "stick it" to the Redskins. Halas utilized every eligible man on his team—33 of them, of which 15 had a share in the scoring.

"It even reached a stage," commented *New York Times* columnist Arthur Daley, "that the Bears passed for one point after touchdown by way of variety and by way of adding to Washington's humiliation."

Those few Redskins' optimists remaining at the start of the second half had their hopes snuffed almost immediately when the Bears scored only 54 seconds into the third quarter. "This was simply dreadful," noted Daley. "The only question before the house was whether the Bears could score more points when they were on the offensive or when Washington was on the offensive. It was a fairly close competition. Chicago with the ball outscoring the Redskins with the ball, seven touchdowns to four."

The on-field architect of the massacre was Bears quarterback Sid Luckman, a graduate of Columbia University. Perfection may have been Luckman's downfall. He performed so expertly in the first half that Halas benched him in the second in an effort to curb the scoring.

The Redskins best opportunity to make a game of it developed after Chicago's Bill Osmanski raced 68 yards for the first touchdown. Taking the kickoff, Washington moved to the Chicago 26-yard line, whereupon Bob Masterson of the Redskins attempted a field goal. The boot— from the 32-yard line—missed, and everything was downhill for the Redskins after that. Had Masterson kicked the ball between the uprights,

Washington would have trailed only 7–3 and might have been able to rebound, but such was not to be the case.

The Redskins' other futile threat was marshaled in the second quarter, when, after recovering a Bears' fumble, Washington marched to the Chicago 18-yard line. Once there, however, the sorrowful Redskins lost the ball on downs.

One of the most disheartening aspects of the Washington crusade was the failure of Redskins quarterback Sammy Baugh to make even the slightest imprint on the attack. Typical of Baugh's failure was a third-quarter pass to Jimmy Johnston that was intercepted by Hampton Pool and ultimately led to another touchdown.

Nobody suffered more from the humiliation than Washington's coach Ray Flaherty. "There was no Redskin hero outside of Flaherty," wrote Daley, "who had to sit on the bench and absorb it all, too much a beating for so fine a gentleman and coach. The Bears had 33 heroes. . . . At the end the Redskin band played 'Should Auld Acquaintance Be Forgot?' If said acquaintance is the Chicago Bears, it should be forgot immediately."

**When did a rare ejection from
a football game cost Jimmy Brown a chance
at a regular-season scoring title?**

In 1965, Jim Brown and Gale Sayers battled through the final game of the season in the race for the National Football League scoring title. At kickoff time, Sayers led Brown, 21 touchdowns to 20.

Brown momentarily tied Sayers for the lead when he scored an early touchdown in the first half of the Cleveland Browns–St. Louis Cardinals game in St. Louis. But Brown lost any chance to go ahead of Sayers when he was ejected for fighting late in the first half. Meanwhile, Sayers scored a touchdown in his team's 24–17 loss to Minnesota at home, to win the 1965 scoring title with 22 touchdowns. In addition, Sayers's 22 scores established a National Football League touchdown-making record, breaking the old mark of 20, which had been set by the Baltimore Colts' Lenny Moore.

**Pearl Harbor Day, December 7, 1941,
also was a significant day in football history.
Can you recall any of the gridiron events
that took place on the day that President
Franklin Delano Roosevelt said
"will live in infamy"?**

It was, to begin with, the final day of the regular National Football League season, a time when special ceremonies are conducted by some teams. The seething rivals of New York City—the Brooklyn Dodgers and New York Giants—had a game at the Polo Grounds in Manhattan. Weeks earlier, the Giants' management had proclaimed December 7 as "Tuffy Leemans Day," on behalf of the club's superb running back.

More than 55,000 fans jammed the horseshoe stadium in Harlem to honor Leemans and cheer their favorites. Before the opening kickoff, Tuffy received a silver tray inscribed by his teammates and $1,500 worth of U.S. Defense Bonds. Then the Dodgers, led by Pug Manders, proceeded to demolish their rivals, 21–7.

Meanwhile, an equally enthusiastic audience of 27,102 rooters filed into Griffith Stadium in Washington, D.C., where the hometown Redskins were preparing to play the Philadelphia Eagles. Here, too, pregame festivities were planned—but of another sort. Al Blozis, a Georgetown University tackle and shot-put champion, presented traveling bags to three of the Eagles players and one Redskin, each of whom had graduated from Georgetown. It was a gift from the student body.

There were no distractions at Wrigley Field in Chicago, where the Bears were hoping to defeat their crosstown foe, the Cardinals. A win for the Bears would mean the opportunity for them to tie the idle Green Bay Packers for the Western Division championship and force a play-off.

The Giants, who had finished atop the NFL's Eastern Division, were favored to topple their interborough enemies, but the upstart Dodgers were not to be denied and actually had a shutout going until late in the fourth quarter. By contrast, the Cardinals–Bears encounter was tense and close. For a while, in the final quarter, it appeared that the Cards were close to an awesome upset, but the Bears rallied for two touchdowns in the final five minutes to pull out a 34–24 victory. Likewise, the Washington–Philadelphia match had fans on the edge of their seats—especially in the fourth quarter, when Sammy Baugh, the peerless Redskin quarterback, tossed a pair of touchdown passes enabling Washington to annex a 20–14 win.

To football fans, Pearl Harbor day was filled with ironies, many of them tragic. For example, Al Blozis, the collegian who delivered the traveling bags on behalf of the Georgetown alumni, graduated to the football Giants and eventually was named an All-League tackle. Like many of his teammates, Blozis eventually joined the army. Leading a patrol during the final months of the war, Lieutenant Blozis was killed by German fire in the Vosges Mountains of France.

Equally ironic was the manner in which spectators watching the football warriors learned about the war breaking out in the Pacific. At both the Polo Grounds and Griffith Stadium, the news of the Pearl Harbor attack was transmitted over the Western Union sports ticker located in the respective press boxes. The standard sports transmission was interrupted during the game to permit the announcement of the Japanese aerial assault. Although the news instantly spread throughout the press box, it was withheld from the fans on the field.

Within minutes the bulletin was flashed over the radio, so that thousands of listeners obtained word of the attack before those at the Polo Grounds. "The public address announcers at the two games did not relay to the crowds the reports that were coming in on the wire services," commented Richard E. Goldstein in *The New York Times*. "But a spectator did not need a portable radio to tell him that momentous events were in progress."

Before any of the NFL games had been concluded a series of tension-bathed announcements spread through the various stadia. Most of them were directed at high-ranking members of the military, who were told to report to their senior officers or to their command posts.

"Not relayed over the loudspeaker at the Redskins game," noted Richard E. Goldstein, "was the report of a phone call for Edward A.

Tamm, assistant to the director of the Federal Bureau of Investigation. Employees at the message center in Griffith Stadium knew the location of Tamm's seat and sent a courier to bring him to the phone. J. Edgar Hoover, in New York for the weekend, was patched into the connection. The caller was Robert L. Shivers, the special agent in charge of the FBI's Honolulu office.

"Shivers reported the chaos erupting around him and then placed his phone next to an open window so Tamm and Hoover could hear the sounds of explosions for themselves."

The war changed the entire complexion of professional football. There was talk—just as there had been regarding baseball and hockey—of closing down the leagues altogether for the duration of hostilities, but it was concluded that morale would be best served by keeping the various pro sports alive.

However, some teams were so decimated by the military draft that traumatic changes were made among the NFL members. A 1943 union of the Philadelphia Eagles and Pittsburgh Steelers resulted in the Pitt-Phil Steagles. In 1944 a marriage between the Steelers and Chicago Cardinals took place. This merger was labelled the "Card-Pitts."

Despite the loss of key players, the NFL survived and provided employment for innumerable players who ordinarily might have been earning a living in other professions. Previously retired aces such as Ken Strong and Bronko Nagurski were pulled out of mothballs by the

Giants and Bears, respectively. It was, as they say, a whole new ball game. That "Day of Infamy" forever changed the complexion of the world and, with it, the face of the NFL.

When did a team win a game 15 minutes after it was apparently over?

In 1943, during his first campaign as head coach of Ohio State University, Paul Brown enjoyed an experience that few coaches can match.

The Buckeyes were deadlocked at 26–26 in a wild battle with the University of Illinois. As play went into the final seconds, Ohio had the ball on the Illini 28-yard line. A pileup developed on the next play and the crowd surged onto the field as the final gun sounded.

Brown followed his team into the dressing room for the usual postgame press conference. While it was in progress, the referee stuck his head through the open door.

"The game isn't over," the referee said. "You still have one more play. Illinois was offside on the last one."

The Ohio State players hurriedly re-dressed and rushed back to the field, where remnants of the crowd were milling around. Some knew what had happened and tried to guess what the final play would be. Coach Brown knew. He had already told John Stungis to attempt a field goal, although Stungis had never kicked one before.

"There's nothing to it, John," Brown told him. "I never missed a field goal in my life!"

So Stungis kicked a placement. It wasn't an elegant kick—it was a wobbler that barely had enough strength to clear the crossbar before collapsing. But it was fancy enough to delight Stungis, who had raced into the clubhouse shouting in celebration of the 29–26 Ohio victory: "Coach, I'm even with you. I've never missed a field goal either!"

Brown grinned. "John," he replied, "you're one up on me. I've never even tried one!"

Can you name the NFL defensive end who ran 66 yards *the wrong way* for a touchdown, giving the opposition two points instead of scoring six for his team?

On October 26, 1964, at San Francisco's Kezar Stadium, the Minnesota Vikings' Jim Marshall, a fine defensive end, was involved in the memorable play.

While playing the San Francisco 49ers, Marshall watched as quarterback George Mira attempted a pass to Bill Kilmer. The receiver caught the ball and then fumbled it. Marshall scooped the ball up and after avoiding a few early tackles, was out in the open, heading toward the goal line with only a few of his teammates pursuing him.

Desperately, his Viking teammates shouted

to him, but Marshall heard nothing as he sprinted into the Vikings' end zone. The defensive end had run the wrong way and, instead of scoring six points on a touchdown for his team, he had scored two points on a safety for the 49ers.

As a humiliated Marshall explained later, "I saw my teammates running down the sidelines, and I thought they were cheering for me."

Marshall was lucky. The Vikings won the game, 27–22, and his teammates were able to make light of, rather than cry over, his mistake.

No doubt fans will be wondering if the Bill Kilmer who fumbled the ball and caused the play to occur, is the same Billy Kilmer who later quarterbacked the Washington Redskins' famed Over the Hill Gang. The answer is yes. Kilmer was a halfback as well as a quarterback during the early part of his career.

One of the most brutal games ever played on a pro football field was the opening contest in 1976 between the world champion Pittsburgh Steelers and the Oakland Raiders. Can you recall any of the vicious plays from that game?

Dirty tactics on the gridiron received a lot of ink during the 1976 season as the result of crippling injuries to several quarterbacks, receivers, and runners. The furor began on opening day, when the world champion Pittsburgh

Steelers renewed their hate campaign with the Oakland Raiders at the Oakland-Alameda County Coliseum.

During the contest Pittsburgh's splendid receiver Lynn Swann absorbed two separate, vicious hits on pass plays—one by Oakland defensive back Jack Tatum that knocked him dizzy; and a karate-type forearm smash on the back of the head by another defensive back, George Atkinson. Atkinson's hit gave Swann a concussion, forcing him to leave the game. "It wasn't until I hit him that I saw that [Steeler running back] Franco Harris had the ball," Atkinson stated afterwards. "I wasn't trying to hurt him, but I have no regrets."

Steelers head coach Chuck Noll was furious with the Raiders' "game plan" and criticized them for representing "a criminal element." The "criminals" received their penalties a week later, when Commissioner Pete Rozelle fined Tatum $750 and then slapped Atkinson with a $1,500 fine. Noll was fined $1,200 because of a rule in the NFL's constitution prohibiting public criticism of other teams.

Is football in danger of becoming too violent? Never, according to George Atkinson, who reflects the views of most of Sunday's heroes: "If they want to take aggressiveness out of the game, we'll wear flags in our pockets the next time we play."

Who was the first player to block a field goal attempt while standing more than 40 yards from the kicker?

R. C. Owens, a wide receiver for the Baltimore Colts, had been a superb basketball player and high jumper in college. When he played with Y. A. Tittle on the New York Giants, they combined to perfect the "alley-oop" play, in which Owens would outjump the defensive team to catch a high floater, much like a rebounder in basketball.

Since both the crossbar and a basketball hoop are ten feet off the ground, Owens knew that he could block an occasional field goal. The Colts were playing the Washington Redskins when Owens got his first chance to attempt the block. Bob Khayat of the Redskins tried for a field goal from the Baltimore 40 yard line. Owens waited under the crossbar. The kick went off and as the ball began its descent, Owens flexed his legs and prepared for his goaltending assault. His fingers made contact with the ball and he tipped it away—a blocked field goal from a remarkable 40 yards away.

The 1963 Philadelphia Eagles were a tough team, but the team's most violent episode involved one Eagle against another in a fight that was termed the most violent incident in the history of the National Football League. Who were the players involved in the fight?

The eruption took place on the day after President John F. Kennedy was assassinated. Despite the assassination, NFL Commissioner Pete Rozelle ruled that all games would be played the coming Sunday. Several Eagle players disputed Rozelle's decision. Bill Quinlan started the argument by saying that "the game wouldn't have to be played if it wasn't for Pete Rozelle, that guinea bastard!" Rozelle was not of Italian extraction, but defensive back Ben Scotti was. Scotti took exception to Quinlan's statement and retorted, "I don't know what Rozelle is, but I don't like that word, *guinea.*"

"He's a guinea bastard," Quinlan repeated.

Scotti replied, "Cut it out or there'll be trouble."

Quinlan backed down, but his road roommate, John Mellakas, a 260-pound center, began needling Scotti.

"So he said *GUINEA,* so what?" Mellakas said. Scotti again asked that the expression *guinea* not be used.

Mellakas snapped, "You're not so tough, Scotti, and I've had as much out of you as I'm going to take."

"You want to fight?" Scotti asked.

Mellakas replied, "Anywhere you want."

The two would have squared off in the dressing room, but coaches told them to cool it. The 26-year-old Scotti, who weighed 184 pounds, and 30-year-old Mellakas returned to their hotel room, locked the door, and began to fight. When the dust cleared, Mellakas lay unconscious with black eyes, a broken nose, and several missing teeth. Scotti had cut his hands so badly on his teammate's face that he needed surgery on his right hand. He had a cut tendon on his ring finger, and needed 15 stitches.

Scotti eventually was cut by the Eagles, after being suspended and put on injured waivers. Mellakas was fined but later returned to the varsity.

What teams have their training camps located in Florida?

Unlike baseball, the only pro football teams with training camps in the Sunshine State are the Miami Dolphins, the Tampa Bay Buccaneers, and the New Orleans Saints.

Which NFL stadium holds the largest number of people?

The Silverdome in Pontiac, Michigan, holds up to 80,638 fans.

Where was Vince Lombardi born?

In Brooklyn, New York, on June 11, 1913.

Who was selected in 1979 as quarterback for the Professional Football Writers Association's All-Pro Team?

Dan Fouts of the San Diego Chargers.

What team has super turf in its stadium?

The New England Patriots are the only NFL team to play on Super Turf.

Which NFL stadium holds the smallest number of people?

Metropolitan Stadium in Minnesota seats only 48,446.

On November 10, 1968, the Chicago Bears'
Gale Sayers, one of the finest running backs
in professional football, suffered a
crippling knee injury that permanently altered
his career. Who was the player responsible
for injuring Sayers?

It was the ninth game of the season for the
Bears, who held a 24–6 lead over the San Francisco 49ers at the time of the accident. Quarterback Virgil Carter called for a pass to Sayers,
who took the short toss and moved downfield.
As he cut to the inside to avoid defensive tackle
Kevin Hardy, cornerback Kermit Alexander hit
Sayers with a low rolling block just at the point
where his cleats were anchored in the turf.
Sayers' knee took the brunt of the blow, which
caused the ligaments to tear, and he was hospitalized and then subjected to lengthy therapy
in an effort to repair the damage. Eventually, he
returned to action after rehabilitation, but he was
never the same. A sad footnote: When Sayers
was injured, he was off to his best National Football League season, with 856 yards rushing in
only nine games, well ahead of all other NFL
runners.

**Who was the first football player
to gain nationwide recognition?**

Football's answer to Babe Ruth was Harold
"Red" Grange.

Nicknamed Red because of his flame-col-
ored hair, Grange brought national attention to
football. Grange displayed his superior talents in
high school, yet failed to win a college scholarship. He arrived at the University of Illinois
campus after having spent the summer earning
$38.50 a week to help pay for his tuition. Intent
on majoring in business and trying out for the
basketball and track teams, Grange found himself on the freshman football team as a result of
a fraternity pledge.

In his first game, Grange caught coach Bob
Zuppke's attention when he scored two touchdowns. As a sophomore, Grange was given number 77, a figure that soon became ingrained in
the minds of college football fans. Playing
against a tough University of Nebraska team,
Grange galloped for touchdowns of 35, 60, and
12 yards. By season's end he had scored 12
touchdowns and had amassed more than half of
the Illini's total points. He gained 1,296 yards,
was named to Grantland Rice's All-American
team, and was the leader of Illinois' undefeated,
national collegiate championship team.

As a junior at Illinois, Grange took on the
trappings of a superstar. On October 18, 1924,
the University of Illinois dedicated its new mil-
lion-dollar stadium, and on that day Grange

established himself as one of the greatest open-field runners of all time.

The Illini's opponents that day were the feared University of Michigan Wolverines, who had been Big Ten co-champions the previous year and had won 20 straight games. Just before game time Michigan's athletic director, Fielding "Hurry Up" Yost threatened to pull his team off the playing field. Yost was outraged that Illinois gridders had emerged from the clubhouse (to the cheers of 67,000 fans) with one of their players not wearing socks.

Yost began screaming, "Zuppke's cheating. It's illegal and we won't play." But the officials found no rules against not wearing socks.

Yost, who had derided Grange before the game, contemptuously ordered that the opening kickoff be directed right at Red. This was a mistake. Taking the ball on his own 5-yard line, Grange zigzagged down the field. At one point all 11 Michigan tacklers were in front of him, but still he invented ways to get around them. He ran into the end zone unhurt and untouched.

Minutes later Grange raced 67 yards from the Illinois line of scrimmage to score again. Twice more—once for 56 and once for 44 yards—Grange scored in the first quarter, giving him a total of four touchdowns in the first 12 minutes of play. By the end of the first half he had run 262 yards on only four carries.

In the second half Grange ran 15 yards for one touchdown and threw for another. By the day's end he had gained a total of 402 yards and scored five touchdowns against a Michigan team that had not allowed as many as four touchdowns in one game in five years. He earned his new nickname, "The Galloping Ghost." One journalist wrote that Grange had given "the most spectacular single-handed performance ever delivered in a major game."

Grange came East only once in his career, and on that day he made believers out of any skeptics there may have been among the East Coast writers who had never seen him play. Running against the Eastern champions, the University of Pennsylvania, Red gained 363 yards, scoring three touchdowns and setting up one other.

Red Grange was the first football player to be considered a genuine American star in the Babe Ruth/Jack Dempsey mold. He was as famous as anyone in the United States (including renowned pilot Charles Lindbergh, whose own special talents were also capturing American hearts at that time). Today, many believe that pro football first gained acceptance in American households when Grange entered the professional ranks.

**In 1940 he won the Heisman Trophy and
the Maxwell and Walter Camp Awards.
He was often compared to the immortal
Red Grange, but World War II interrupted
his professional career. Who was this potential
superstar?**

Tom Harmon. In 1940, Harmon, a Michigan running back, captured the three prestigious awards and was named a consensus All-American as well. During his 24-game college career, Harmon scored 33 touchdowns and kicked the points after touchdown and two field goals, for a total of 237 points. That exceeded Grange's record, and at the time was the best scoring record in Big Ten history.

**He was a consensus All-American at the
University of Alabama in 1934, then was named
All-Pro nine times during his ten-year career.
He was inducted into the Pro Football
Hall of Fame in 1963 and was voted to the
modern All-Time All-American Team and
the All-Century Team. Who was this
National Football League super talent?**

Don Hutson led the NFL in scoring five times, pass receiving eight times, interceptions in 1940, and field goals in 1943. He caught 99 touchdown passes in his career, including 17 in 1942. He spent his entire pro career with the Green Bay Packers.

Who was the first coach to win 100 games in the span of a decade?

Don Shula turned the trick during the 1970s. Shula, a five-time winner of the National Football League's Coach of the Year award, was responsible during that period for steering the Miami Dolphins to the league's first undefeated, 17-game season in 53 years.

Shula prepared for coaching while playing on the John Carroll University team. Not only did Shula play, but he also took notes while on the sidelines, studying and soaking up every phase of the game. He turned pro with the Cleveland Browns, then played for the Baltimore Colts and, finally, the Washington Redskins. His teammates described him as a "scholar of the game" who "seldom made the same mistake twice."

Shula rates himself as having been a "marginal player." After seven years as a pro, he became an assistant coach in college and, following that, took a similar position with the Detroit Lions.

Shula made himself known in 1963, at age 33, when he was named head coach of the Baltimore Colts. During seven seasons in Baltimore, he ran up the highest percentage of wins for any coach over a comparable period of time.

His first attempt to win the Super Bowl, against the New York Jets in 1969, failed. A year later he severed his roots in Baltimore and reblossomed in Miami as head coach as well as vice-president and part-owner of the then weak Dolphins. Shula rebuilt the team in a hurry and in 1972 led the young Dolphins to the Super Bowl. Though they lost to the more-experienced Dallas Cowboys, 24–3, the Dolphins rebounded in 1973, to defeat the Washington Redskins, 14–7, in the pigskin classic and end the season undefeated.

Although he boasted the best winning percentage of all pro football coaches—including Vince Lombardi—Shula was assailed by critics who claimed after his Super Bowl losses to the Jets and Cowboys that he couldn't win the big game. The victory over the Redskins and a follow-up win over the Vikings in the 1974 Super Bowl, 24–7, forever silenced the armchair quarterbacks and critics.

When and where was the first Super Bowl played? Who were the opponents?

Super Bowl I, played in Los Angeles on January 15, 1967, pitted the American League champion Kansas City Chiefs against the National League champion Green Bay Packers. Green Bay won, 35–10, thanks to a spectacular performance by reserve pass catcher Max McGee, who at one point never expected to play in the game at all.

Early in the game Green Bay's starting receiver Boyd Dowler injured his shoulder. Mc-

Gee, a veteran of 12 seasons, entered the game as Dowler's substitute. McGee launched his assault on the Chief defense by taking a Bart Starr pass for a touchdown. The Chiefs counterattacked on Len Dawson's pass to Curtis McClinton. At halftime the Packers led, 14–10, and it appeared that the second half would be a dogfight to the end.

It wasn't. Defensive back Willie Wood intercepted a Dawson pass only three minutes into the third quarter to set up a touchdown run by Elijah Pitts from the 5-yard line. Suddenly it was 21–10 Green Bay. In no time at all, the Chiefs were forced to punt, whereupon Starr took to the air and found McGee waiting in the end zone. McGee juggled the ball for a moment, but his sure hands latched on to the pigskin for a touchdown. Now Green Bay was up, 28–10. Soon, Pitts scored again to ensure that the Packers would become the first Super Bowl champs.

Ironically, four of the touchdowns were scored by reserves McGee and Pitts. Most notable was that McGee had caught only four passes all season.

Who was the "Heisman" of the Heisman Trophy?

The award was named after John Heisman, one of football's outstanding innovators. Heisman developed the center snap, added "hep" and "hike" to our vocabulary, had the forward pass legalized, schemed the hidden-ball trick, and invented the scoreboard.

The New York Jets pulled off one of the biggest upsets in Super Bowl history when they beat the Baltimore Colts. What was the score of that game?

Quarterback Joe Namath led the Jets to a 16–7 victory over a stunned Baltimore team. Prior to the game, Baltimore was a 7–1 favorite in the opinion of the oddsmakers, but the Jets, and particularly Namath, were confident they would emerge victorious. "I guarantee it," Namath was heard to say. He did.

When Hall of Famer Sammy Baugh was drafted by the Washington Redskins he received what then was a fabulous bonus. What was it?

Baugh had Redskins owner Preston Marshall in a bind because the future Hall Of Famer also was offered a baseball contract with the St. Louis Cardinals. Marshall was forced to pay Baugh more than he ever paid a Redskin rookie. "Sam," Marshall said, "I'll give you five thousand dollars to play for us next season. Plus a five-hundred-dollar bonus. You'll be the highest-paid player on the team." Baugh accepted the offer and soon proved worth the investment.

Washington Redskins back Larry Brown was one of the best runners in the early 1970s. He was drafted by the Redskins out of Kansas State University and became a starter in his rookie year. In what round was he drafted and who was the Redskins' head coach at the time?

Brown was drafted eighth and was greeted at training camp by the most famous and feared head coach in pro football, Vince Lombardi. Brown had not been a standout collegian but displayed determination to Lombardi right from the start of camp. The coach liked to employ the "nutcracker" drill on his recruits; its purpose was to test a runner's heart. Two padded dummies were lined up four feet apart; between them were two linemen, and a defensive back stood five yards behind. Two runners were asked to break through to the other side. But many backs simply told Lombardi they couldn't do it (those being the players who were cut). Lombardi would make a back repeat the drill over and over again. The one back who consistently broke through was Larry Brown.

Lombardi was hard on Brown—as he was on all of his players—but he liked the back so much that he started him in that rookie season and Brown responded by gaining 888 yards for the year. Lombardi also discovered that Brown had a hearing problem. When the ailment was properly diagnosed, it was discovered that Larry was totally deaf in one ear. Lombardi had Brown's helmet fitted with a special hearing device so that he could properly hear plays being called. Lombardi died the following year.

The Masonic Boys Home of Fort Worth, Texas, made a significant contribution to the ferocity of pro football in the 1950s. How?

This relatively obscure institution produced two of the toughest players ever to don shoulder pads—both in the same decade. Tex Coulter of the New York Giants and Hardy Brown of the San Francisco 49ers may not have made it to the Hall of Fame, but both are bona fide National Football League legends.

Coulter, an offensive guard and tackle who could be persuaded to switch to defense when necessary, worked at his hard-guy image. Don Paul, Los Angeles Rams linebacker, said he could always tell which lineman would be playing against Coulter simply by picking out the one holding his head in his hands before the game.

Once, when a last-minute lineup switch moved native Oklahoman Stan West across the line from Coulter, West caught Paul looking at him in the Rams' locker room. "Well," he roared, "I'm not going to let this blankety-blank intimidate me!"

On the first play of the game, West hauled off and hit Coulter in the face. Paul said he could hear Coulter's deep bass voice: "So that's the way it's going to be, huh, Okie?"

On second down, a sweep to the other side of the field, Don Paul heard a weird, terrifying scream. He looked over and there was West, holding his mouth as blood trickled down the front of his jersey. Coulter's retaliatory shot had knocked West's teeth through his upper jaw.

Y. A. Tittle once called Hardy Brown "pound for pound, inch for inch, the toughest football player I've ever met . . . he was so tough, he was damn near illegal." While not an imposing physical specimen at 6'0", 180 pounds, Brown nevertheless betrayed an inner frenzy that drove him to destroy the opposition with a vengeance. From 1951 through 1955, Hardy Brown was the scourge of pro football.

Some of Brown's most notorious "accomplishments" include knocking out the entire starting backfield of the Washington Redskins, sparing only quarterback Harry Gilmer. That was in 1951. In the same season he tackled Glenn Davis head-on as Davis plunged through the line. Brown pounded Davis, tearing ligaments in the running back's knee. The injury hastened Davis's retirement.

Brown's most devastating tackle of the 1951

season occurred during a home game at Kezar Stadium. Never one to risk arm tackling, Brown used to crouch down and spring upward into his victim, driving his shoulder into the ball-carrier's head. This time, he hit Pittsburgh's Joe Geri so hard that one of Geri's eyes popped out and was literally hanging by a tendon. The incident did nothing to increase Brown's popularity or diminish his legend.

The 1950 National Football League Championship was won by the Cleveland Browns in the final seconds by a score of 30–28 over the Los Angeles Rams. Who scored the winning points for the Browns?

Lou Groza, the Browns' peerless field-goal kicker, provided the decisive points with a 16-yard field goal with less than half a minute left in the contest. Cleveland was trailing, 28–27, with only one minute and 45 seconds left and the ball on their own 32-yard line. Otto Graham, the Browns' quarterback, immediately ran for 14 yards. He then completed a 15-yard pass to Rex Bumgardner, who stepped out of bounds, thus stopping the clock. Graham then ran three more plays, finally putting the ball on the 10-yard line, setting Groza up for the field goal.

The Green Bay Packers Beat the Dallas Cowboys, 21–17, for the 1967 NFL championship on a frigid afternoon in Green Bay. How did the Packers score the winning touchdown?

With the temperature hovering below the zero mark and only 13 seconds left on the clock, the Packers trailed the Cowboys 17–14. At this point Green Bay quarterback Bart Starr called a quarterback sneak and took the ball and squeezed into the end zone from the 1-yard line for the victory.

Few in the shivering crowd of 50,961 had expected Green Bay to go for the touchdown. The Packers had run out of time-outs. It was third down, but if Starr's attempted score had failed it was unlikely that enough time would have remained for a field-goal attempt. Most viewers had expected Green Bay's coach Vince Lombardi to play for the tie by opting for a field goal attempt and take his chances in sudden-death overtime.

Lombardi countered that he "couldn't see going for a tie and making all those people in the stands suffer through a sudden-death period in subzero temperatures."

In *Instant Replay*, his best-selling diary of Green Bay's season, guard Jerry Kramer wrote of the final play: "I came off the ball as fast as I ever have in my life. I came off the ball as fast as anyone could. In fact, I wouldn't swear that I didn't beat the center's snap by a fraction of a second. I wouldn't swear that I wasn't actually offside."

And when he saw that Starr had made it safely and without obstruction into the end zone Kramer felt that "it was the most beautiful sight in the world, seeing Bart lying next to me, and seeing the referee in front of me, his arms over his head signaling the touchdown."

After Don Chandler's conversion had given the Packers their 21–17 lead, Dallas still had time to run two plays. Both were pass attempts that failed. The hometown fans engulfed the field and their victorious players.

At last, on one of the coldest days in NFL history, what turned out to be the last NFL championship game that Vince Lombardi coached in was over.

Who is known as the "Father of American Football"?

A former Yale captain and a founder of the Intercollegiate Football Association—the precursor of the Ivy League—Walter Camp wrote the first football rule book ever published and introduced (among other things) the 11-man team, the quarterback position, downs, yards-to-go, signal calling, and the scoring system.

Camp also created the All-American Team. Beginning in 1889, Camp began compiling a list of 11 gridders whom he considered the greatest players of that particular season.

Camp died in 1924, at the age of 65, while attending a rules committee meeting.

By the end of an October day in 1974 the Packers, 49ers, Lions, and Giants all had new quarterbacks. How did all the changes come about?

In Los Angeles, the Rams had quickly become disenchanted with their starting quarterback, former San Diego Chargers' star John Hadl, and decided to go with the younger arm of James Harris. Thus, Hadl was traded to Green Bay for the Packers' number one, two, and three draft picks in 1975 and their number one and two choices in 1976.

Meanwhile, in San Francisco, the 49ers were acquiring journeyman quarterback Norm Snead from the Giants for two high draft picks in 1975 and 1976. Having acquired one quarterback, the 49ers dispatched their own Joe Reed to the Lions.

And in Dallas the Cowboys were sending disgruntled Craig Morton to the Giants for New York's number one pick in 1975. Morton had said he was tired of playing behind the Cowboys' All-Pro quarterback Roger Staubach.

How did an official's error almost deprive Miami Dolphins' running back Mercury Morris of a 1,000-yard season in 1972?

After National Football League commissioner Pete Rozelle viewed films of the October 22, 1972, game between the Dolphins and the Buffalo Bills, he ruled that a nine-yard loss charged against Morris should have been charged as a fumble against the Dolphins' quarterback Earl Morrall.

On the play Morrall attempted to pass to Morris but the ball was tipped by Bills defensive lineman Dave Washington and recovered by Buffalo. At the time, the officials ruled that the play was a lateral and charged the yardage loss to Morris. But Commissioner Rozelle, the ultimate authority, ruled otherwise.

Morris needed Rozelle's help. The ruling gave him exactly 1,000 yards for the season.

Why were the Chicago Bears forced to forfeit a sixth-round draft pick in 1976?

Commissioner Pete Rozelle ruled that the Bears had violated the National Football League's embargo on attempting to sign World Football League players. Along with the forfeiture, Rozelle reprimanded then Bears coach Jack Pardee, who had been negotiating with six players he had coached the previous season, while with the WFL's Florida Blazers.

Bears general manager Jim Finks charged that it was he who was actually guilty of the violation, not Pardee. "Our anticipation that the embargo would be lifted sooner was incorrect. We were guilty of the violation and agree completely with the commissioner's action," said Finks.

Can you name any of the significant rules changes made in 1906?

• Teams were allowed four downs to advance ten yards.

• The forward pass was legalized and an end zone was established for passes over the goal line.

• Kickoffs were moved back from midfield to the 40-yard line.

• Seven men were required to be on the offensive line but were not allowed to interlock arms for blocking or running interference.

• Playing time was reset at four periods of 15 minutes each and the present scoring system was finalized.

What numbers did Jim Brown and O. J. Simpson have in common during their National Football League careers?

Their uniform numbers! Both Brown and Simpson wore number 32 on their jerseys.

Charlie Hennigan, a wide receiver who ranks among the top 20 receivers in National Football League history, once said about another wide receiver, "Once in a lifetime a player comes along who alone is worth the price of admission." Who is the player in question?

Lance Alworth of the Houston Oilers and later the San Diego Chargers.

Alworth was the first to surpass one of the most long-lasting pass-catching records, that of catching at least one pass in 96 consecutive games, breaking Don Hutson's NFL record.

What is extra-special about the behavior of Houston's football fans?

Oiler fans carry blue and white pom-poms, use megaphones, and sing the team's fight song, which sounds like a polka. Most of the spectators wear some shade of blue. One woman even dyed her hair to match the shade of the team's Columbia blue jerseys. Then there is the ubiquitous Oiler slogan, "Luv Ya Blue," seen in newspapers and magazines, on billboards, T-shirts, bumper stickers, and scrawled on the sides of bridges. More than 150 souvenir items, including neckties, bandanas, hats, baby grand pianos, belts, ceiling fans, automobiles and tractors, carry the "Luv Ya Blue" tag line.

Houston's tunes include "The Oilers Fight Song," "Luv Ya Blue," "Super Bowl Itch," "Big Bad Earl," "The Ballad of Bum and the Boys," "Snake Bite," and the "Oiler Cannonball."

**Who was the superfoot in
"The Saga of Superfoot?"**

In the early 1970s, three well-to-do Bostonians named Eddie Andelman, Mark Witkin, and Jim McCarthy conducted a humorous radio talk show called *Sports Huddle*. The trio were given to zany behavior now and then, and on one particular night they were despairing over the New England Patriots' failure to produce an adequate placekicker to follow the aging Gino Cappelletti. Andelman, Witkin, and McCarthy decided to rectify the problem. Thus began "The Saga of Superfoot"—or, to put it another way, the search throughout the British Isles for a first-rate placekicker, American-style.

Here, in Andelman's own words, is what happened:

We decided to take quick action. I requested that our producer call the air freight terminal of British Overseas Airways in London, England. We have made bizarre calls like this many, many times, but none ever had such significant repercussions as the call to London. This launched the now memorable "Search For Superfoot." As pursuits go, only Stanley's chase after Livingstone in darkest Africa is even comparable.

The phone rang twice and then, from clear across the Atlantic Ocean, we heard a voice: "BOAC, may I help you?"

"Certainly," I said in my most proper English accent. "This is Lord Andelman, distantly descended from the Northumberland Guards. Would you kindly tell me, old chap, if you could arrange for the New England Patriots, American football team, to send to England a giant box of one hundred American footballs and two human-type scouts; and if so, how much it would cost?"

While the BOAC gentleman wondered at the other end what in heaven's name I had in mind, I further explained that our football team badly needed a European soccer-style kicker. One thing you have to say about the British, they never lose their cool. The polite BOAC clerk heard me out, allowed that it was an unusual request but added that his company could and would comply.

Happily, our listeners got the message. Many called in, pointing out how other European soccer players such as Pete Gogolak and Bobby Howfield had managed to succeed in the American pro league. Within a week a wave of enthusiasm had engulfed the BOAC people as well as our own station manager, Jim Lightfoot. In no time at all Mr. Tony Linney, BOAC's man in Boston, had agreed that the airlines would go along with the promotion. One question remained: What would the Patriots think of the idea?

Billy Sullivan, owner of the ball club, would be decisive, but we were apprehensive of him. After all, we had just completed 18 months on the air, most of which were riddled with darts puncturing the Patriots' image. We had constantly kidded the Patriots, charging, among other things, that bread and water was their official training food. "See the movie, *Holding*—the official film of the Patriots' offensive line," we'd joke. We merely were reflecting the fans disenchantment with the Patriots' frugality: the failure to obtain top draft choices of value, poor playing conditions, and numerous other gripes which made the Pats easy pickings.

While wondering how to approach Sullivan, three miracles took place. First, Joe Kapp signed to play for Boston, and the New England fans were delirious with joy. Next, the $6.6 million stadium for the football team, Schaefer Stadium, was progressing well enough to assure a good press. Finally, Clive Rush, a very bad coach, was canned by the Pats. The whole town was talking about finishing in last place so that the Patriots would have the first draft pick for next year, Stanford's Jim Plunkett. So, for weeks, the three of us wondered how we would approach Sullivan, fearful that he would tell us to go jump in the Charles River.

Finally, we did meet, and Sullivan was the very soul of kindness and understanding. He liked the Superfoot idea and wondered what he could do to help. "Billy," I stammered, "aren't you even mad at us a little?"

I was almost disappointed when he told us how much he enjoyed our show and that anyone who can't laugh at himself a little can't enjoy life. Billy Sullivan not only was with us but provided 100 official footballs as well as training films and a tryout for the winning contestant plus the second- and third-place finishers.

But the next day it appeared that our idea would evaporate as fast as a Patriots' lead. The BOAC home office rejected the idea because, as the national airline of England, law forbade it from indulging in such a promotion. But Tip Pyle, our BOAC man in New York, saved the day. He suggested that the London *Daily Mirror* would like to join such a promotion since they previously had run contests for the nastiest dog in England, not to mention a formal ball for charwomen. Pyle's tip was a good one, and the *Daily Mirror* joined the search for Superfoot.

We decided that there would be a series of preliminary competitions scattered throughout Great Britain, then two semifinal rounds and a grand finale with 12 contestants participating. Altogether we eliminated 560 contestants prior to the semifinals. Frank "Bucko" Kilroy, director of player personnel for the Pats, had scouted the prospects and returned home telling us he knew who would win. As it turned out he was right.

All of New England now sat back and awaited the results of the finals, which were staged at the U.S. Air Force base in Upper Heyford. The competition started at the 35-yard line. An American Air Force sergeant held the ball and the kickers had little difficulty from that short range. At 45 yards out, the field was trimmed to seven. At 50 yards it was trimmed to three.

Up until this point a burly English Army sergeant, Peter "Tug" Wilson, held the lead. But at 55 yards, on came a 21-year-old English bricklayer named Michael Walker. Just then rain began to fall and the temperature dropped. Nevertheless, Walker sent the ball through the uprights. Even when he missed on a subsequent try, Walker showed that he had the distance. While a deluge of rain drenched the field, Mike Walker won the contest. Tug Wilson was second, and a 24-year-old beer salesman, Albie Evans, finished third. All three were signed by the Patriots for a July tryout. The "People's Kicker" had at last been found.

Now it was July and the real test. The Patriots opened training camp with 12 place-kickers. In no time at all Tug Wilson was cut from the squad. Ouch! Somehow he had never regained his contest form, and soon returned to his army unit in Germany. Unfortunately Albie Evans, our second man, developed a groin pull during his tryout and was eventually also cut. This was tragic because he could punt as well as placekick and had proven that his distance was incredible.

Our winner, Mike Walker, was one of the final three kickers retained by the Patriots, along with Charlie Gogolak and Gino Cappelletti. According to Upton Bell, the Pats' general manager, Walker was one of the finest athletes he ever encountered: 6' 1", 190 pounds, capable of running 40 yards in 4.6 and immensely strong. Rommie Loud, one of the Pats' top scouts, believed that Mike bordered on the superior. Gino was cut, and retired. It was now between Gogolak and Walker. Gogolak got the job and Superfoot was relegated to the taxi squad. It was generally agreed that he still needed practice since his soccer orientation never accounted for the monstrous National Football League line. Also, he needed coaching.

The fact that he didn't make it was a bit of a personal blow to us, but the contest was rewarding if only to prove that there is fun in sports.

Well, our archenemies, the sports purists and the Boston sportswriters, were now given the opportunity to laugh at our feeble efforts. To add to our depression, we had been fired by the Westinghouse Broadcasting Company, which turned out to be a lucky break, since the various pressures exerted by management were impossible to cope with if our creed of "for the fan" was to be followed. Then Upton Bell called and asked us to his office. He requested that we give him our word to keep in confidence what he was about to relate, and naturally we did. Bell explained that the report of "Superfoot" returning to England because he was homesick was a ruse. Actually, the Pats had no kicking coach, but they were bringing Mike Walker back the following spring to work with Ben Agajanian, at which time Walker would announce his unretirement. To make a long story short, it was hard to take the abuse and barbs about "Superfoot" all winter, but we did since we had given our word. By this time we were hired by WEEI and were back on the air.

Walker, of course, made the 1972 Pats' team, and we were as proud as three fathers with a newborn son. Unfortunately, Mike missed five games and kicked well below his capacity throughout the year, but he showed great promise. It was a great source of personal satisfaction to know that every time "Superfoot" trotted out onto the field he aggravated the Boston sportswriters and the purist rooters who said it was stupid for the three of us to search England for Superfoot.

Who were the "Four Horsemen" of Notre Dame and how was their nickname coined?

Notre Dame's "Four Horsemen" were Harry Stuhldreher, Donald Miller, Jim Crowley, and Elmer Layden. They were so nicknamed on October 18, 1924, by Grantland Rice, a sportswriter for the New York *Herald-Tribune*. Rice, who was to become known as the dean of American sports journalists, covered the Army–Notre Dame game at the Polo Grounds in Manhattan. Thanks to the superior effort of Notre

Dame's backfielders, the Fighting Irish defeated a powerful Army team, 13–7.

Rice was so impressed with their performance that he began his story as follows:

> Outlined against a blue-gray October sky, the Four Horsemen rode again. In dramatic lore they are known as Famine, Pestilence, Destruction and Death. These are only aliases. Their real names are Stuhldreher, Miller, Crowley and Layden. They formed the crest of the South Bend cyclone before which another fighting Army football team was swept over the precipice at the Polo Grounds as 55,000 spectators peered down on the bewildering panorama spread on the green plain below.

One of the ironic aspects of that game was the fact that Notre Dame coach Knute Rockne benched the Four Horsemen at the start of the game, using almost entirely a second-string cast. As a result Army dominated the early part of the game. But Rockne seemed to be holding his aces in reserve and when he finally did send them to the front line they proved their worth. Here is how Grantland Rice described Notre Dame's first touchdown march of the day:

> On the first play the fleet Crowley peeled off 15 yards and the cloud from the west was now beginning to show signs of lightning and thunder. The fleet, powerful Layden got six yards more and then Don Miller added ten. A forward pass from Stuhldreher to Crowley added 12 yards, and a moment later Don Miller ran 20 yards around Army's right wing. He was

on his way to glory when Wilson, hurtling across the right of way, nailed him on the 10-yard line and threw him out of bounds. Crowley, Miller and Layden—Miller, Layden and Crowley—one or another, ripping and crashing through, as the Army defense threw everything it had in the way to stop this wild charge that had now come 70 yards. Crowley and Layden added five yards more and then, on a split play, Layden went ten yards across the line as if he had just been fired from the black mouth of a howitzer.

Grantland Rice's description of the Notre Dame backfield immortalized the Fighting Irish football team and converted Crowley, Miller, Layden, and Stuhldreher into household words.

The story of the game also lifted Rice to a level rarely achieved by sportswriters. "Rice," commented another accomplished journalist, Stanley Frank, "remained supreme in the technique of lush leads and giving rich elaboration to a story while, by no means incidentally, weaving all the essential facts into his colorful patter.

Consider Rice's ending to his Four Horsemen story: "The Army has no cause for gloom over its showing. It played first-class football against more speed than it could match. Those who have tackled a cyclone can understand."

**How did collegian Jeff Miles
set an unofficial record for versatility
in 1980?**

Jeff Miles, a junior at Juniata College in Huntingdon, Pa., performed above and beyond the call of duty in a 35–10 victory against Albright.

Miles, a 5'10", 175-pounder, started at his usual position in the defensive backfield. Then he switched to flanker and later moved to running back. When Juniata's starting quarterback was injured, Miles took over that position—one he never had played.

On his first play as signal caller, he ran 16 yards for a touchdown. On his team's next possession, he threw his first pass and completed it for 19 yards and another touchdown. Later he tossed an 80-yard scoring pass.

For the day, Miles ran 15 times for 102 yards and completed four of 10 passes for 107 yards. In his spare time, he returned a punt for 21 yards. Not bad for a defensive back!

**How far did the shortest touchdown pass
ever recorded in professional football history
travel?**

The shortest pass thrown for a touchdown was a two-incher thrown by Eddie LeBaron to Dick Bielski in a Dallas Cowboy–Washington Redskins game on October 9, 1960.

Can you recall the professional football record for the most consecutive games in which a receiver has caught a touchdown pass?

The record for catching touchdown passes in consecutive games is 11, and it was accomplished twice. Elroy "Crazylegs" Hirsch of the Los Angeles Rams snared 11 during the 1950–51 season. Buddy Dial of the Pittsburgh Steelers did it again, in 1959–60.

Who holds the National Football League record for the most pass receptions in a game?

Tom Fears caught 18 for the Los Angeles Rams against the Green Bay Packers on December 3, 1950, gaining 189 yards in the process.

Name the quarterback who holds the record for most seasons leading the National Football League in passing?

For six years Sammy Baugh of the Washington Redskins led the NFL in passing. Baugh was tops in 1937, 1940, 1943, 1945, 1947, and 1949.

**Who holds the career record
for most interceptions and most yards
returned on interceptions?**

Emlen Tunnell of the New York Giants produced 79 career interceptions. Tunnell, who starred for the Giants until his retirement in 1961, returned the pick-offs for a record 1,282 yards.

Why is Paul Bryant referred to as "Bear"?

Paul Bryant, the University of Alabama head football coach for more than two decades, earned the nickname after an episode in which he wrestled a bear. Louise Bryant, the coach's sister, tells the story: "A man paraded a bear up and down the main street with a sign on it that read 'Paul Bryant Will Wrestle This Bear.' He offered Paul five dollars and to us that was one heck of a lot of money. They wrestled, but Paul who was only about 10 at the time, never received his money."

**The New York Giants won the 1934
National Football League championship game
over the Chicago Bears, 30–13. However,
the Giants scored 27 of those points in the
final ten minutes of the game. The turnabout
took place as the result of a strategic "change"
the Giants made. What was it?**

The 1934 championship game was among
the most bizarre in pro football history. The
game took place on a frigid day in front of
35,050 fans.

The Giants and the Bears were pitted
against each other, as they had been the previous year, only this time on the Giants' turf.
On this day the field resembled an ice rink, as
the ground had frozen over solid.

New York couldn't maneuver against Chicago and the Bears, who as two-time champions,
were heavily favored to repeat, were leading,
13–3, in the fourth quarter. Now was the time
for Giants coach Steve Owen to borrow a tip
from Ray Flaherty, one of his players. "Steve,"
said Flaherty, "it may sound crazy but one day
when I was playing for Gonzaga the ground was
just like this. We switched from cleats to basketball shoes and got some traction."

At halftime Owen ordered Giants clubhouse
attendant Abe Cohen to borrow some basketball
sneakers from the Manhattan College gymna-
sium. With ten minutes left in the game the
sneakers had arrived. The Giants called a time-
out and began trying on the sneakers while the

incredulous Bears looked on. Finally, the sneaker-clad gridders took the field.

Giants quarterback Ed Danowski completed a 28-yard touchdown strike to Ike Frankian. The extra point was good. Now the score was 13–10, Chicago. In no time at all New York regained the pigskin. Giants running back Ken Strong immediately scooted 42 yards for another score. The Giants were ahead to stay and romped to victory thanks to several pairs of basketball shoes.

**Who was the first football coach ever
to diagram plays on paper and charts?
(Hint: He later became the president of
the United States.)**

Woodrow Wilson, the 28th president of the United States, also was the first football coach—while at Princeton University—to chart plays and formations with the use of graphs.

Wilson was a successful coach. He never ranted or raved. He would lecture his players on the virtues of decency and good sportsmanship.

**How was the Houston Oilers' slogan,
"Love Ya Blue," coined?**

It was created by Donna Agner, a Houston medical secretary who first scrawled the slogan on a sign at the Oilers' fieldhouse facility. In time it became the rallying call for the Oilers.

**Bubba Smith, one of the greatest
defensive linemen in football, also was
extremely superstitious. What unusual ritual
did Smith perform before every game?**

Bubba Smith donned his uniform in a most unusual manner. Before he would put on his pants he would lace his left shoe. Bubba performed this ritual before every game. Billy Ray Smith, who played alongside Bubba in the Baltimore defensive line, once asked, "Do you know how hard it is to pull your pants on over a size fourteen-and-a-half shoe?" Bubba obviously was unimpressed.

A National Football League coach once said
of a defensive lineman, "He's so strong
that he can tackle the runner and search him
for the ball at the same time."
Who was the coach and the player in question?

The coach was Don Shula, who made the
observation about Chicago Bears rookie Dick
Butkus in 1965. Butkus had just caused a fumble
and recovered two others in a 13–0 Bears victory
over Shula's Baltimore Colts. The 6'3", 245-
pounder enjoyed an excellent rookie season, including five interceptions. However, he was
beaten out in the Rookie of the Year balloting
by teammate Gale Sayers, who had an equally
sensational season, setting a league record with
22 touchdowns. Butkus continued to improve
while the Bears faltered. Club owner George
Halas described Butkus as "the greatest Chicago
lineman in 30 years."

Name the first two Southwest Conference players
to be named All-American, and the year
in which they were chosen.

Although the Southwest Conference boasted
innumerable stars in its first 15 years of exis-
tence, it failed to obtain nationwide attention. It
wasn't until 1929 that two players from the conference were recognized as All-Americans. They
were Arkansas end Wear Schoonover and Southern Methodist University tackle Marion Ham-

mon. In time the South was recognized as a top breeding ground for football prospects.

Why was the Kansas City Chiefs participation in Super Bowl I, especially sweet for Chiefs' owner Lamar Hunt?

Lamar Hunt was especially pleased with his team's Super Bowl appearance because he organized the American Football League, after being rebuffed by the National Football League. Hunt wasn't pleased with the final score though, as the Green Bay Packers trounced the Chiefs 35–10.

Who was the first coach to win championships in both the old National Football League and the American Football League?

Weeb Ewbank won back-to-back titles in 1958 and 1959 as head coach of the Baltimore Colts in the National Football League. In 1969, he led the New York Jets of the American Football League to the AFL's first Super Bowl championship.

A graduate of Miami of Ohio, where he was a quarterback, captain of the baseball team, and a member of the basketball team, Ewbank began his coaching career at Miami as an assistant coach, spending 14 years there. In 1943 he became a member of the Great Lakes Naval Training Station team and after the war was named backfield coach and head basketball coach at Brown University.

Weeb next moved to Washington University in St. Louis as head football coach, and his two-year record of 14–4 was the best the school had enjoyed in 30 years.

In 1954, when he was named Baltimore's head coach, he took a Colt team that was one of the worst in football and within six seasons produced two championship clubs.

Some of Ewbank's former players and associates became successful head coaches in pro football in their own right, including Don Shula, Chuck Knox, and the late Don McCafferty.

Weeb said it was impossible to select one game as his most memorable as a pro coach. He insisted upon picking two games. One was the 1958 championship play-off game, when the underrated Baltimore Colts defeated the New York Giants, 23–17, in sudden-death overtime for the NFL title; the other was the 1969 New York Jets' upset of his former Baltimore team (three-touchdown favorites), 16–7, for the first American Football League victory in a Super Bowl.

**Middle linebacker Sam Huff was a mainstay
of the New York Giants' defense for many years.
But Sam almost walked out of
the Giants' camp in his rookie year. Why?**

Huff and teammate Don Chandler had not been expecting the harsh treatment they encountered at the Giants' camp. Head coach Jim Lee Howell betrayed a high decibel count, as did Vince Lombardi, the Giants' assistant defensive coach. The two got homesick and one night decided to leave for home. Fortunately, they were talked out of leaving by assistant coaches Lombardi and Ed Kolman.

**Notre Dame met Army for the first time
on November 13, 1913. What was the
final score of the game?**

Notre Dame set the stage for a good rivalry by battering Army by a score of 35–13.

Notre Dame quarterback Charlie Dorias and receiver Knute Rockne were the greatest passing battery the game had seen at that time. Up until then most of the game was kept on the ground, with teams running the ball on almost every play. The toughest team would usually win. Dorias and Rockne had other ideas, however. The two were roommates and perfected the forward pass, developing it as a new major weapon.

The scoring began on Notre Dame's first

possession, with three passes in five plays, and it was the beginning of a long afternoon for Army. Before the game was over Dorias had racked up 243 yards on forward passes alone and Notre Dame scored an easy victory.

Columbia University has not had the most successful teams in college football history, but in 1934 the Lions scored one of the greatest upsets ever in a Rose Bowl game. Name the team Columbia defeated and the final score of that game.

During the 1934 season Columbia was a surprise in the East. The Lions scored victories over formidable opponents such as Navy, Penn State, and Syracuse. At the time, however, Eastern football was taken lightly by the rest of the country, and when Columbia was pitted against Stanford in the Rose Bowl, no one gave the New Yorkers a chance.

Stanford was a powerhouse, with aces Bones Hamilton and Bobby Grayson in the backfield and a strong line. They were heavily favored at game time.

The field was more like a swamp for the start of the contest, and this would work to Columbia's advantage. While the Stanford backfield could not get on track, Columbia took full advantage of the conditions in the second quarter, scoring the only touchdown of the game on a 17-yard run by Al Barabas. The extra point was good and Columbia held on to win, 7–0. It was the Lions greatest victory ever.

Name the former University of Southern California quarterback who started at safety for the Green Bay Packers in Super Bowl I.

Willie Wood. Wood quarterbacked USC in 1959. He was the first USC player to start in a Super Bowl.

Who are the six coaches who have winning records in Super Bowl play?

Chuck Noll, Pittsburgh (4–0); Vince Lombardi, Green Bay (2–0); Weeb Ewbank, New York Jets (1–0); Don McCafferty, Baltimore (1–0), John Madden, Oakland (1–0) and Tom Flores, also of Oakland (1–0).

Only one team failed to score a touchdown in a Super Bowl game. Which team was it and what year?

Miami failed to score a touchdown in Super Bowl VI which was played in 1972. The Dolphins lost the game, 24–3, to the Dallas Cowboys.

What do Max McGee, Bill Miller, Cliff Branch and John Stallworth have in common?

The quartet are the only four players to have caught two touchdown passes in a single Super Bowl game. Branch snared his while playing with Oakland in Super Bowl XV, Stallworth in Super Bowl XIII with Pittsburgh, Miller with Oakland in Super Bowl II and McGee with Green Bay in Super Bowl I.

Who is the only athlete who has played in a Super Bowl and a World Series game?

Tom Brown batted only .147 as a first baseman and outfielder in 61 games with the Washington Senators in 1963. Brown played defensive back with Green Bay in Super Bowls I and II. He finished his career in 1969 with the Redskins.

Who is the only Dallas Cowboy to have caught touchdown passes in more than one Super Bowl game?

Butch Johnson caught touchdown passes in the 1978 and 1979 games.

Name the only former Notre Dame quarterback who has thrown a touchdown pass in a Super Bowl game.

Daryle Lamonica. The former Fighting Irishman threw for both of Oakland's touchdown passes against Green Bay in Super Bowl II.

Can you name the teams in the Big Eight, Big Ten, and Pacific Ten Conferences?

The Big Ten includes Michigan, Michigan State, Northwestern, Wisconsin, Indiana, Ohio State, Illinois, Purdue, Iowa, and Minnesota.

The Big Eight comprises Missouri, Nebraska, Colorado, Oklahoma, Oklahoma State, Kansas, Kansas State, and Iowa State.

The Pacific Ten includes Oregon, Oregon State, Washington, Washington State, Arizona, Arizona State, California, Southern California, UCLA, and Stanford.

The Rose Bowl, played every year on New Year's Day, features a team from the Big Ten playing a representative of the Pacific Ten. Prior to 1978, the Pacific Ten was known as the Pacific Eight; in 1978, Arizona and Arizona State were admitted to the conference, at which point it became the Pacific Ten.

Through the 1979 season, how many National football players have rushed for more than 1,000 yards in their rookie year?

No fewer than 12 players have rushed for more than 1,000 yards in their rookie season. The first was Beattie Feathers of the Chicago Bears who rushed for 1,004 yards in 1934. Others include:

1962 Cookie Gilchrist, Buffalo Bills....................1,096

1968 Paul Robinson, Cincinnati Bengals...............1,023

1971 John Brockington, Green Bay Packers............1,105

1972 Franco Harris, Pittsburgh Steelers................1,055

1973 Lawrence McCutcheon, Los Angeles Rams.........1,097

1974 Don Woods, San Diego Chargers.................1,162

1977 Tony Dorsett, Dallas Cowboys....................1,007

*1978 Earl Campbell, Houston Oilers....................1,450

1978 Terry Miller, Buffalo Bills.......................1,060

1979 Otis Anderson, St. Louis Cardinals...............1,605

* Starting in 1978, 16 games were played during the regular season instead of 14.

What player was so valuable his contract provided that his brother-in-law be given a job, for $10,000 a year, as a scout?

The New York Jets wanted this player so badly that they signed him to a four-year contract plus a bonus of $200,000. Three brothers and one brother-in-law also were given jobs as scouts for another $10,000 apiece a year, not to mention receipt of a green Lincoln Continental. The deal, with all fringe benefits, totaled close to $430,000.

The man the Jets wanted so badly was none other than Joe Namath. At the time some critics suggested that Namath was being overpaid and that the American Football League looked foolish in the process. But Joe proved them wrong when he guided the Jets to a Super Bowl victory in 1969 over the heavily favored Colts.

On a Saturday afternoon in 1929, Yale and Army played at the Yale Bowl in what turned out to be one of the most significant upsets in college football history. What happened?

Yale had been a football powerhouse during the early part of the 20th century but had lost its might in the 1920s. In contrast Army had a solid team and the Cadets were expected to win easily.

But Yale's Albie Booth—dubbed a "144-pound dynamo"—put on a one-man show to lead the Elis to a 21–13 upset over Army. With Army leading, 13–0, Booth spearheaded a 32-yard drive. Albie personally scored the touchdown that put Yale on the board. Then he dropkicked the extra point. A short time later Booth repeated the same script, only this time he led the team in from 35 yards out and again dropkicked the extra point. The 80,000 fans at the Yale Bowl looked on at first in disbelief, and then responded with thunderous cheers.

The peripatetic Booth wasn't finished. He received an Army punt on Yale's 35-yard line and ran it back 65 yards for a touchdown, thereby earning himself a permanent place in the hearts of Yale's football fans.

Name the National Football League team that dispenses "Dude of the Week" prizes to its fellow teammates?

During the 1980 football season, spirits were so high on the Cleveland Browns that each week they nominated one player for the Doug Dieken "Dude of the Week" prizes. These included a 1″ × 5½″ life-size picture of diminutive Browns' punt receiver Dino Hall, an 8″ × 10″ semiaction picture of Browns' fullback Calvin Hill running with the ball, and a two-week course at Cleveland Crosby's School of Self-Motivation. (Crosby, once the University of Arizona defensive end, was the Browns' second-round draft pick in 1980 training camp but was cut early in the preseason.)

Asked to play baseball for the Yankees
and to box professionally, this all-around
athlete was an All-American lacrosse player
and once even won the high-jump
at a college track meet while warming up
for a lacrosse game. Yet he opted
for pro football and went on to become
the man many consider the finest runner ever
to set foot on the gridiron. Who was he?

Jimmy Brown. As a teenager, Brown was
asked by Casey Stengel to play baseball in the
Yankees' organization. Shortly after graduating
from Syracuse University, Brown was offered
$150,000 to become a heavyweight boxer. He
played nine seasons for the Cleveland Browns,
rushing for 12,312 yards, a team mark that still
stands.

Who was the former Alabama quarterback
who followed Ken Stabler at that position
and went on to become a star third baseman
for the Boston Red Sox?

Butch Hobson.
Through 1980, Hobson had hit more than
90 home runs.

Hall of Famer Gale Sayers played in
the same collegiate backfield as a pitcher
who went on to win more than 100 games
in the major leagues. Who is the pitcher?

Steve Renko.

Louisiana State University's quarterback
in the 1974 Orange Bowl against Penn State
pursued a career as an infielder with the
California Angels before being killed
in a car crash. Do you know who he was?

Mike Miley.

Who was the former
New York Yankees' catcher who finished third
in the 1960 Heisman Trophy balloting?

Jake Gibbs.

Name the quarterback who led the Bills
to their first championship
and later served in Congress?

Jack Kemp was the key to the Bills' first
American Football League title, in 1964. The
championship was the first ever for the city of

Buffalo dating back to the All-America Football Conference in the 1940s.

Kemp who was claimed from San Diego in 1962 for the $100 waiver price, retired in 1969, and eventually became a U.S. representative from the Buffalo area. The quarterback was also mentioned as a possible candidate for the Republican vice-presidential nomination in 1980.

**In the 1964 college football draft,
Joe Namath was selected by the
American Football League's New York Jets.
Which National Football League team also
selected him?**

The St. Louis Cardinals picked Namath ninth in the opening round.

**Name the wide receiver who was drafted
in the 12th round, finished second one season
in receiving, and lost a record 22 contact lenses?**

Bob Trumpy.

This 6'6", 220-pound receiver wasted no time in confronting the trainer of the Cincinnati Bengals, Marv Pollins, about his need for contact lenses. The first day of training camp for the newly formed Bengals in 1968 was the day Trumpy informed the trainer about his condition.

"I wear contact lenses," the tall rookie said, "and I can't see a thing without them."

"That's fine," said Pollins. "What about it?"

"Well," replied big Bob, "out at Utah they had an extra pair for me and the trainer always carried them in his bag. You'd better get me an extra pair."

"We'll have to talk to the boss about that," replied Pollins.

Pollins spoke to owner Paul Brown, who said, "You tell him that if he makes the team, we'll buy him an extra pair."

After the trainer relayed Brown's answer, the confident rookie said, "You go back and tell him to order those contacts because I'm making this club."

And he did. Despite being drafted in the 12th round, Trumpy made the team with no problem. Later on he said, "I had to attract attention the minute I hit the camp. I knew all along I was going to make the ball club, but 12th-round draft choices have a way of being forgotten if you don't let them know you're around." Trumpy certainly did let them know he was around. He was not only the team's best tight end, but the team's best wide receiver.

In 1968, the Bengals were last in the league in touchdowns via the pass, converting only eight. The former All-American high school performer in both football and basketball began the 1969 season on the wrong foot. Shortly thereafter, Trumpy suffered a bruised rib, bumped knee, and other nagging injuries that hampered his performance. Nevertheless, 1969 was his big year. With rookie quarterback Greg Cook providing the leadership, Trumpy established himself among the league's top receivers. In the second game of the season he caught three passes for 118 yards, including a 78-yard touchdown. The following week he hauled in an 80-yard scoring strike.

Although Bob fell victim to a hunting accident worth 15 stitches on his leg, it did not interrupt his outstanding season. The following Sunday, Trumpy had the greatest game of his pro career. He caught five passes for 159 yards, three of them for touchdowns.

Despite an aching wrist, Bob pulled in another touchdown pass the following week and went on to a total of nine, one more than the entire Bengal squad had managed for the entire year. At one point Trumpy actually led the league in average yards gained on receptions, before yielding the crown to Oakland's Warren Wells. Still, Trumpy's 22.6-yard rate was one of the finest figures for receivers in NFL history—especially for a tight end.

**Which top football stars were suspended
for a season for betting on
National Football League games?**

Detroit Lion Alex Karras and Paul Hornung, the Green Bay Packers' Golden Boy who
led the NFL in scoring three years, were
suspended on April 17, 1963. The two players
had admitted betting on their own teams and on
other games in which they were not involved.

Karras and Hornung weren't the only cul-
prits. Five other Detroit players were fined
$2,000 each for betting on one game and the
Detroit club was fined a total of $4,000. The five
players fined were Joe Schmidt, Wayne Walker,
John Gordy, Gary Lowe, and Sam Williams.

**Some of the most bizarre characters
inhabited the 1960–61 New York Titans,
and they were involved with some zany incidents,
too. Can you recall any of them?**

Hubert Bobo, a linebacker with two bad
knees, was one of the offbeat characters on that
Titan team in the American Football League.
Curly Johnson, the Titan punter at the time,
remembered one incident: "We were playing
cards one night on the plane trip coming back
from a game. Bobo was angry about something
so he was punching every guy who dealt too
slowly." When asked whether he did anything
about Bobo's fury, Johnson replied, "Do any-

thing? I was the most nervous one there. It was my deal next."

On another occasion, the Titans were making a 1960 preseason trip from Abilene, Texas, to Mobile, Alabama. Titans owner Harry Wismer decided that the 900-mile jaunt would be cheaper by overnight train than by plane, since he would also save on the dinner bill (Harry would book 8:00 P.M. flights for West Coast trips to avoid paying meal money). Harry assured the team that they'd be in an air-conditioned train all the way.

Of course, there was no air conditioning and the trip through the late summer Texas evening proved to be a nightmare. There wasn't even any hot water for shaving. By the time the train reached Mobile, players were virtually out of clean clothes. Alas, when the Titans arrived in Mobile, they learned that a parade in their honor had been scheduled that day.

What was unusual about Don Maynard when he first appeared at the New York Titans Training Camp in 1960?

Maynard was a New York Giants' reject by way of Canada. The Titans didn't like his sideburns or his cowboy boots, which were a decade ahead of their time.

Maynard's teammate Larry Grantham recalled: "I'll never forget the first time I ever laid

eyes on Don. He was sitting there with a big hat
on and cowboy boots. He looked like he was
waiting for the rodeo to start. He had blue jeans
on, and a belt with a big brass buckle that had
number thirteen on both sides. And written
across the face of it was 'Shine.' That was his
nickname in college."

Despite his radical appearance, sartorially
speaking, Maynard managed to play 13 seasons
as a professional.

**Which venerable college football stadium
was known as the "Ground Gainer's Mecca,"
and why?**

Syracuse University's Archbold Stadium
shall go down in history as America's foremost
showplace of the run. It was in this stadium
that the Orangemen would run and run and run.
When Syracuse got the ball during the years
1953–67, the Orangemen more often than not
ran with it.

The Syracuse running craze started in 1953,
when a 16-year-old freshman named Jim Brown
hit campus. It finally began to let up in 1967,
when a brawling half-track of a fullback named
Larry Csonka walked away from the halls of
Ivy to pursue a Super Bowl with the Miami
Dolphins.

In between, coach Floyd "Ben" Schwartz-
walder, who coached football at Syracuse for 24

years, gave the ball to such fleet players as Ernie Davis, Jim Nance, and Floyd Little. Together with Brown and Csonka, the five gained a career total of 11,720 yards, or almost seven miles.

The fans in upstate New York loved every mile of it, whether it was from the powerful, generally short bursts of Csonka and Nance, the uncanny broken-field long gainers of Little or Davis, or the awesome thrusts of Brown. The luck that the players enjoyed was passed along to each other, as was jersey number 44, which was first worn by Brown.

These were the big names. All of them, with the exception of Davis (who died of leukemia shortly after graduation), went on to further glory and yardage records in professional football. Overlooked in the excitement were others who excelled in the Syracuse backfield: Jim Rildon, who turned to defense in the pros; Art Baker, who opted for the Canadian League; and German immigrant Gerhard Schwedes, a number one draft pick of the Boston Patriots in 1960 who simply didn't make it. Syracuse truly was a mecca of the run!

Name the Houston kickoff returner who "walked on" to the Oilers' roster at the start of the 1978 season.

Johnny Dirden, a 26-year-old Houston cement company worker, parked his rig outside the Oilers' headquarters, walked into then head coach Bum Phillips' office in his dusty overalls, and told Phillips that his college experience consisted of seven kickoff returns and that his last game was played in a rodeo camp. "But," added Dirden, "I want a tryout." Phillips laughed. Finally, the coach suggested that Dirden run the 40-yard dash. Johnny did it in 4.5 seconds. The incredulous Phillips asked the brash intruder to do it again. Dirden repeated a 4.5 40-yard dash and landed a job as a kick returner. Not only that, but Johnny finished the 1978 season as the American Football Conference's second-leading kickoff returner with a 33.5-yard average.

This man began his professional coaching career at the age of 33, making him the youngest National Football League head coach ever. Who is he?

Don Shula, who began coaching the Baltimore Colts in 1963 after working as an assistant coach for the Detroit Lions under George Wilson. In 1964 the Colts won the NFL West Title. One of Shula's finest teams was the undefeated Miami Dolphins of 1972.

During the 1940s Army boasted two superb running backs known as "Mr. Inside" and "Mr. Outside." Do you recall their names?

Felix "Doc" Blanchard and Glenn Davis were Mr. Inside and Mr. Outside, respectively, and they enjoyed three superb seasons (1944–46) with the Cadets of West Point.

Between them, Davis and Blanchard scored 89 touchdowns and averaged 8.3 yards a carry. During that span, the Black Knights never tasted defeat, winning 27 and tying one.

What was the all-time high score recorded in collegiate football?

On October 7, 1916, Georgia Tech defeated Cumberland, 220–0. One Rambling Wreck backfield star scored 18 touchdowns all by himself!

When he was owner of the New York Football Yankees, Dan Topping once offered to trade his entire team for a certain quarterback and build a new team around that player. Who was the quarterback?

The Chicago Bears' Sid Luckman, one of the most accomplished T-formation quarterbacks ever to take a snap from center, was the recipient of Topping's admiration.

What do the initials "O. J." stand for in O. J. Simpson's name?

Orenthal James—not Orange Juice.

What was football's first offensive formation and why was it banned?

The play was called "The Wedge." To launch it, a team of blocking lineman would hang onto suitcase handles sewed to the pants of the teammates in front and thunder together down the field, with the ballcarrier in the center of the group. In 1905 this formation caused 18 deaths among college and high school players and eventually was banned.

In football's earliest days a runner was not counted as being officially down until he did what?

A runner first had to admit he was down before the down counted. The refusal to yell "down" could be injurious, if not fatal, to a ballcarrier!

In what year was the American Football League organized and what were the original teams?

The AFL was created in 1960 with the following teams: Boston Patriots, New York Titans, Dallas Texans, Denver Broncos, Los Angeles Chargers, and Oakland Raiders.

The Chargers moved to San Diego in 1961. The Titans became the Jets in 1963. The Texans moved from Dallas to Kansas City, where they became the Chiefs. The Patriots, after years of camping around the Boston area, finally settled in Foxboro, Massachusetts, as the New England Patriots. The American and National Leagues merged in 1966, and by 1977, 26 teams were playing under the banner of the National Football League!

Who holds the record for average yards gained rushing in a game?

No, it's neither Jim Brown nor O. J. Simpson—Marion Motley holds the record. Motley, a fullback with the Cleveland Browns, averaged 17.09 yards rushing in a 1950 contest against the Pittsburgh Steelers. Motley carried 11 times for 188 yards.

How was the Green Bay Packers franchise born?

In August 1919, Earl L. "Curly" Lambeau, a former college football player at Notre Dame, worked at the Indian Packing Company in Green Bay, Wisconsin. He convinced the company to organize a team, purchase equipment, and loan out its athletic fields for games and practices, in exchange for the team using the nickname "Packers." At that time the team played only on the semiprofessional level.

In their first two years the Packers compiled a 10–1 record and Lambeau was able to convince a Mr. J. E. Clair of the Acme Packing Company (which had taken over from Indian) that the team should turn professional. Wearing the jerseys of the Acme Packers, the team posted a 6–2–2 record in the American Professional Football Association.

In 1922 Association president Joseph Carr discovered that the Packers had recruited and used college players under aliases during the previous season. Carr suspended the franchise and returned the company's $50 entry fee for that year. But a crushed Curly Lambeau managed to save a franchise for the city of Green Bay. He raised the $50 required for a new league franchise by persuading a friend, who was also an enthusiastic football fan, to sell his car. According to author Bert Randolph Sugar, in exchange for this favor, Lambeau promised his friend the "Walter Mittyesque experience of performing one play in Green Bay's opening game."

What was the Chicago Bears' original name?

The Bears originally were named the Decatur Staleys, so-called because they were then backed by the Staley Company of Decatur, Illinois.

In 1921, the Staleys moved into Wrigley Field in Chicago. At the end of that season A. E. Staley declared that he could no longer finance the team and transferred the ownership to George Halas. In order to exploit his relationship with the more famous baseball Cubs, Halas changed the team's name to the Bears.

Name the football player who starred in the films *One Minute To Play* and *Racing Romeo*.

Red Grange.

**Prior to the advent of the Super Bowl,
when was the last time that a championship
professional football game was played
on neutral ground?**

It happened in 1936. The Green Bay Packers
were opposed by the Boston Redskins, soon to
be the Washington Redskins. The championship
game was played at New York's Yankee Stadium. The Packers won, 21–6.

Although the game was played on neutral
ground it attracted 29,545 fans.

**Name the pro quarterback
who was involved in a 1978 speedboat crash
that killed two people.**

In a 1980 interview with *Sport* magazine,
Oakland Raiders' quarterback Dan Pastorini dis-
closed: "It happened so fast, I don't know what
really happened. The boat went out of control
and I was thrown from the seat. It was at
Liberty, Texas. I wound up underneath the deck
of the boat, traveling better than 125 miles an
hour. The boat went into the crowd. It was a
very unfortunate thing but it happens in racing
and I'm deeply sorry. I was named in a lawsuit
that went before a grand jury; it was ruled an
unavoidable accident. Sure, it shook me up and
I stayed away for a while, but I went back to
racing."

Which National Football League team led the league with the most home-grown talent (players acquired via the college draft only) during the 1980 season?

The Pittsburgh Steelers, with 41 drafted players on the roster, boasted more homegrown talent than any other NFL team. The Cincinnati Bengals were second with 37 draft choices, including 23 from rounds one through three. The Bengals and Steelers were two of six NFL teams with 10 first round draft picks on their rosters.

Why was Bronko Nagurski unique among football heroes?

When Bronko (Bronk-o) Nagurski (Nag-ur-ski) attended the University of Minnesota, his varsity team lost only four games, all by two points or less, in his three years of action.

But it's not only the winning or losing that critics remember—it is the versatility of Nagurski. Bronko played every position except center and quarterback and in Nagurski's senior year (1929), Grantland Rice named only ten men to the All-American football team, because *Nagurski was selected at both tackle and fullback.*

There are many stories concerning the strongman. Once, in a 1929 game against Northwestern, Nagurski scored a touchdown from 12 yards out in which every member of the defense took a shot at him and missed. When Bronko ultimately came down in the end zone, it was only because he had run into a pile of lumber.

A similar event had occurred the previous year, when Minnesota played Wisconsin in a game for the Big Ten championship, which Wisconsin only needed to tie to clinch. Bronko had suffered an injury to his spine but insisted on playing with a steel brace.

Late in the game, with both teams scoreless, Minnesota moved close to the Wisconsin goal line. Bronko was given the ball four consecutive times and on the last effort he took it into the end zone carrying six Wisconsin players on his back.

When Bronko joined the Chicago Bears of the National Football League in 1930, he found that his reputation had preceded him. There were stories about how he ran six miles to and from high school every day in his hometown of International Falls, Minnesota (even in the winter) . . . about how he had singlehandedly lifted a truck off an injured man . . . about how he had rescued another man who had been buried under a pole of logs at a sawmill.

Despite the stories, there were many pros who didn't believe Bronko was that strong. These skeptics learned the hard way.

Once, two members of the Pittsburgh Steelers attempted to stop Bronko from reaching the end zone. Result: one player suffered a broken shoulder, the other was knocked out cold. Another time, during a 1933 game against Portsmouth, Nagurski went 44 yards for the winning touchdown, sending two linebackers flying in different directions, running over the defensive halfback, and straight-arming the safety aside before colliding with the goal post and caroming into the brick wall at Wrigley Field in Chicago. "The last guy hit me awful hard," Bronko said after he was revived.

Former Chicago Bears coach George Halas once said, "I assure you that you will not see a more remarkable physical specimen anywhere. He was six feet, two inches, and he weighed 234 pounds and it was literally all muscle, skin, and bone. He didn't have an ounce of fat on him."

Bronko retired in 1938 at the age of 30, over a salary dispute. He returned five years later, when the Bears were thin on tackles. He led the Bears to an NFL championship that year while contributing at tackle and at fullback.

Has any National Football League rookie ever gained 100 yards rushing in each of his first three games?

Six backs have rushed for 100 yards in each of their first two games, but no one has accomplished it in each of his first three games. The six backs who rushed for 100 yards in their first two contests are: Zollie Toth (New York Yankees), 1950; Alan Ameche (Baltimore Colts), 1955; Earl Campbell (Houston Oilers), 1978; Otis Anderson (St. Louis Cardinals) and William Andrews (Atlanta Falcons), 1979; and Billy Sims (Detroit Lions), 1980.

The back who came closest to gaining 100 yards in his first three games was Sims, who fell five yards short of the 100-yard mark on September 21, 1980, against the St. Louis Cardinals after going over 100 yards in each of his first two contests.

A National Football League quarterback was tagged with the dual nicknames "The Polish Rifle" and "Jaws." Who was he?

Ron Jaworski of the Philadelphia Eagles acquired the nickname "The Polish Rifle" during his early years with the Los Angeles Rams, when he displayed a superb arm. The always-confident quarterback later was dubbed "Jaws" because of his high-frequency mouth. Jaworski theorized during his early days with the Rams—when he was the third-string quarterback behind Pat Haden and Jim Harris—that the only way he could obtain recognition was by talking to the media. Mission accomplished for "Jaws," alias "The Polish Rifle."

George Halas, the Hall of Fame coach who developed the T-formation with the Chicago Bears, is credited with several other football "Firsts." Can you name any?

Pro football owes much to the colorful and innovative style of "Papa Bear" Halas. Always in the vanguard of progressive change in the game, Halas's Bears set the standards for many pro teams of the future.

The Bears were the first pro team to hold daily workouts. They were the first to use movies of games for study and analysis of their own and their opponents' mistakes. They were the first team to use a major-league baseball park as their home field and the first to use tarpaulins to protect the gridiron from the ravages of weather. They were the first team to go on a barnstorming tour, the first to have the field announcer name the ballcarrier and the yardage gained or lost on each play, and the first to have an official team song (called, appropriately, "Bear Down, Chicago Bears").

Name two men who were teammates in college and also were winners of the Heisman Trophy in consecutive years.

Playing for Army, "Mr. Inside" and "Mr. Outside" helped their team to an undefeated season in 1944. "Mr. Outside," Glenn Davis, led the nation in scoring with 20 touchdowns and gained an average of 12.4 yards per carry. "Mr. Inside," Doc Blanchard, also had a good year with nine touchdowns and 7.1 yards per carry. Blanchard won the Heisman Trophy the following year, in 1945. In 1946, Davis received his Heisman. Davis and Blanchard formed one of the finest backfield combinations ever to play football.

A professional football player once was served during a football game with a restraining order that prohibited him from continuing to play. Name the player.

On Wednesday, August 28, 1974, John Matuzak, pro football's number one draft choice in the 1973 college draft, jumped from the Houston Oilers of the National Football League to the Houston Texans of the World Football League.

Matuzak played for the Texans that night until he was served on the sidelines with a temporary restraining order that prevented him from finishing the game.

Test your knowledge of football's Hall of Fame. Where is the Hall of Fame located?

Canton, Ohio.

Why is the Hall of Fame located there?

Because Canton is where the American Professional Football Association was organized in 1920. On September 17 of that year, Jim Thorpe, then with the Canton Bulldogs, was elected president of the Association, which totaled 13 teams. The teams kept no formal standings.

Whose idea was the Hall of Fame?

The idea was conceived by a young Canton newspaperman who believed that pro football needed a shrine and that the logical spot was Canton. Canton civic leaders liked the idea and seized what they thought was a golden opportunity. First they gained the official sanction of the National Football League. Then they staged a massive campaign, urging fans to support their efforts by giving their time, talents, and donations so that a modern pro football Hall of Fame could be built. With the help of the many donations, the $1,000,000 House of Champions was completed.

When was the Hall of Fame built?

Dedication of the original two-building complex took place on September 7, 1963.

Why is the Hall of Fame also known as football's "Historical Treasure Chest?"

In addition to containing information about its members, the Hall of Fame also includes the National Football Museum, the National Football Library and the National Football Art Gallery.

How are new members elected to the Hall of Fame?

New members to the Hall of Fame are named by a Board of Selectors, made up of 26 representatives, mostly comprised of outstanding football writers. They meet each year on the day after the Super Bowl. Their selections are officially enshrined in Canton the following summer.

Although the membership ranks of the Hall of Fame comprise mainly National Football League players, induction is not limited to those who roamed the gridiron. Some of those who have been inducted into the Hall of Fame:

Jim Thorpe—halfback, Canton Bulldogs and New York Giants, 1915—26.

Bert Bell—founder, Philadelphia Eagles, 1933

Jack Christiansen—defensive back, Detroit Lions, 1951—58

Otto Graham—quarterback, Cleveland Browns, 1946—55

Cliff Battles—running back, Boston Braves, Boston Redskins, and Washington Redskins, 1932—37

**What was Texas-born president
Lyndon Johnson's favorite football story?**

A young football player from Texas University came to Washington, where he tried out for the Redskins. In his interview with the coach he was asked what he could do.

"Well, gentleman," he said, "there are plusses and minuses. The plusses are I can run one hundred yards in nine-point-six seconds even on a muddy field. I punt seventy yards, and I throw forward passes more than sixty yards against the wind. . . ."

The coach then asked the recruit to list his minuses.

He replied, "Well, seeing as I'm from Texas, I've been known to exaggerate. . . ."

Can you recall which National Football League team was known as the Over-the-Hill Gang?

George Allen's Washington Redskins of the 1970s were tabbed the Over-the-Hill Gang because of their relatively old players. Young gridders were scarce on the Redskins because Allen gave up many top draft choices in order to obtain the experienced players he wanted. Allen explained that he was never sure the drafted player was going to make it, but he already knew what the veteran ballplayer could do.

Allen once said, "I love the phrase 'Over-the-Hill Gang.' These are my kind of players. I have always contended that age means nothing if a man takes care of his body and has the proper attitude and spirit."

Referring to his Redskin team of 1972, which won the NFC championship by whipping the Dallas Cowboys, 26–3, Allen said, "Mainly because of our 'Over-the-Hill Gang,' this was a closely-knit Redskin team. They were not concerned with individual goals. There was a strong feeling of togetherness that was obvious to us during the entire season."

After coming to the Redskins in 1971, Allen became the winningest pro coach in Redskin history and passed the coveted 100-victory mark. Before 1971, the Redskins had had only four winning seasons in the previous 25 years.

Name two presidents of the United States who played football at Harvard.

John F. Kennedy was an end for Harvard's freshman team in 1936 and played for the junior varsity in 1937.

Franklin Delano Roosevelt also was an end and an occasional halfback on the second team at Groton School in 1899, after playing tackle and fullback on the third team in previous years. At Harvard F.D.R. was elected captain of a freshman scrub team in 1900.

Of the 28 National Football League teams, how many wear white in some part of their uniform?

Nineteen teams have at least some white in their uniforms. Those without white: Kansas City Chiefs (red, gold), Miami Dolphins (aqua, orange), Oakland Raiders (silver, black), Pittsburgh Steelers (black, gold), Seattle Seahawks (blue, green, silver), Detroit Lions (silver, Honolulu blue), Green Bay Packers (green, gold), San Francisco 49ers (Forty Niner gold, scarlet), and Washington Redskins (gold, burgundy).

Can you name the team that has scored the most points in combined Super Bowl play?

Although the Pittsburgh Steelers are undefeated in Super Bowl play, Pittsburgh hasn't scored the most points. The Dallas Cowboys are tops with 112 points in their five Super Bowl games. The Cowboys record on Super Sunday is 2–3.

Who was Frank Hinkey and what was his relationship to Yale football?

Frank Hinkey played for Yale before the turn of the century, (1891–94) and was notorious for his rough play.

During his collegiate career, Yale won 52 games and lost only one. In 1893, Hinkey suffered a head-on collision with Jim Blake of Princeton. The Yale ace had to be removed from the field with the help of his teammates. Significantly, Yale lost that day. During Hinkey's four years at Yale, the Elis scored 1,738 points whereas their opponents scored only 25.

Which National Football League team cornered the market on small football players in 1969?

The Kansas City Chiefs could have fielded a backfield composed of Mike Garrett, Warren McVea, and Robert Holmes, and also inserted Noland Smith to run back kicks in 1969. All four gridders had one thing in common: they stood 5′9″ or less.

Exactly how Kansas City cornered the shrimp market isn't clear, except that coach Hank Stram was a famous innovator, civil libertarian, and was 5′7″.

"I think shortness helps," Stram once said. "We get some concealment and we create formations to take advantage of their speed. But it's not something that happened intentionally. I didn't go out to get five-foot-nine backs."

**What ex-football player once played
the character Bashful in *Snow White And
The Seven Dwarfs* at Disneyland?**

Though many players have been called
elves, fleas, or gnats, because of their small size,
only one legitimate dwarf has ever played in
the National Football League: Randy Vataha,
who at 5'8", 176 pounds, looked less like the star
wide receiver for the New England Patriots than
something you would see at Disneyland—which
he was.

Growing up loose and cool in California,
Randy spent his summer college vacations at
Disneyland playing Bashful, one of the Seven
Dwarfs. Vataha later turned his energies to foot-
ball and after being cut by the Los Angeles
Rams, was signed by the New England Patriots.
Vataha rewarded the Patriots in his rookie sea-
son by catching 51 of Jim Plunkett's passes, in-
cluding nine for touchdowns.

**A professional football coach
once was nicknamed the "Lion of Winter."
Who was he?**

Sid Gillman, an epic figure in the history
of the American Football League, often was
dubbed the "Lion of Winter." Gillman had always been a lion of a man in the Vince Lom-
bardi/Paul Brown coaching mold.

Gillman built the San Diego Chargers franchise, coached them through the years of early glory, and kept them alive when the wolf was threatening to have pups on the carpet. Beyond that, he established rigid front-office standards that inspired the rest of the American Football League.

It was not unusual for the lights to be burning in Gillman's office into the early morning hours. On the field, Gillman inspired a common reaction from his players: fear.

A former San Diego fullback once confided that in the locker room before a game, in that moment when each man meditated in his own way, the prayer was never for victory or to be spared serious injury. The prayer was, "Please, God, don't let me be the first one to screw up." The lash of Gillman's angry voice was to be avoided at any cost!

In the 1960s, the National Football League was divided into four divisions, each beginning with the letter *C*. Can you name those four divisions?

They were Capital, Century, Coastal, and Central.

In 1972, ten NFL running backs rushed for more than 1,000 yards. How many can you name?

O. J. Simpson, Buffalo Bills	1,251 yards
Larry Brown, Washington Redskins	1,216 yards
Ron Johnson, New York Giants	1,182 yards
Larry Csonka, Miami Dolphins	1,117 yards
Marv Hubbard, Oakland Raiders	1,100 yards
Franco Harris, Pittsburgh Steelers	1,055 yards
Calvin Hill, Dallas Cowboys	1,036 yards
Mike Garrett, San Diego Chargers	1,031 yards
John Brockington, Green Bay Packers	1,027 yards
Mercury Morris, Miami Dolphins	1,000 yards

George Halas, as owner and coach of the Chicago Bears, had a rule stipulating that any of his players who received an unnecessary roughness penalty would be fined $50. Why did George chip in one time to help a player pay the fine?

The Chicago Bears were playing the Detroit Lions in a close game as the remaining seconds ticked away in the first half. Harry Clark of Chicago carried the ball all the way to the Detroit 5-yard line. A Lion landed on Clark and made no attempt to get up as the clock continued to tick. Bear end Edgar Manske raced over and pulled the Lion off Clark. The official hit Manske with a 15-yard penalty for unnecessary roughness. Although Halas considered the penalty unfair, he enforced his rule and fined Manske. On the sidelines, the Bears chipped in $50 for Manske, and Halas was one of the contributors.

In 1949 the National Football League merged with a four-year-old conference. What was the name of the conference and what agreements were made?

On December 9, 1949, a four-year war between the National Football League and the All-America Football Conference was settled when the two merged. The agreement put an end to one of the most costly wars in the history of professional sports. Club owners had lost millions of dollars in the protracted battle for players and attendance.

The 13 owners agreed that the new league would be called the National-American Football League (or NAF) and comprise the complete ten-club NFL and three teams from the AAFC. The teams from the NFL were the Philadelphia Eagles, New York Giants, New York Bulldogs, Washington Redskins, Pittsburgh Steelers, Chicago Bears, Chicago Cardinals, Detroit Lions, Green Bay Packers, and Los Angeles Rams. Representing the AAC were the San Francisco 49ers, Cleveland Browns, and the Baltimore Colts. The owners then broke the league into two divisions, the American and National, and agreed that the division winners would meet in a world championship game.

Bert Bell, who had been at the helm of the older NFL, became commissioner of the new loop, and Emil R. Fischer of the Green Bay Packers and Daniel Sherly of the Cleveland Browns headed the National and American Conferences, respectively.

Ironically, the man responsible for the merger was Horace Stoneham, owner of the New York baseball Giants. Stoneham started the move when he summoned Bell and J. Arthur Friedlund, an AAFC representative, to a meeting. After round-the-clock conferences, the merger agreement was finally hammered out.

Who scored the most consecutive points in professional football?

During the 1929 football season, Ernie Nevers of the Chicago Cardinals set two records that remain unbroken today. In a game against Dayton, he scored all of his team's 19 points. The following week he again scored all of the points for his team, this time a total of 40, to establish an all-time pro football point-scoring record for one player in a single game. The 59 consecutive points he scored in both games is another record.

**Name the quarterback on the
Chicago Bears' 1933 championship team.**

Carl Brumbaugh was one of the first modern T-formation quarterbacks. Originally, Carl was back-up to starter Joey Sternaman, but in the first regular-season game, Joey was injured. Brumbaugh then took the field and helped the Bears to the 1933 championship.

**Why did Baltimore Colt ace Johnny Unitas
once turn down an opportunity to
appear on Ed Sullivan's TV variety show?**

Immediately following the 1958 NFL title game, which the Colts had won in sudden-death overtime, a representative of Sullivan's popular TV program asked Unitas to appear on that night's show to "take a bow."

Unitas would have received $750—no paltry sum for a quarterback in 1958—*if* he had decided to go on. But appearing on TV that night would have meant remaining in New York while the rest of the team headed back to Baltimore without him. Unitas decided that he could do without the $750.

Sullivan's agent was incredulous. "You've won the championship. You don't have to go back to Baltimore now," he shouted.

"I know," Unitas replied calmly, "but being with the players tonight is more important to me than $750."

115

When was the first "Sudden-Death" overtime in an NFL championship game played?

It happened in 1958, in a game that is regarded by many as the greatest ever played in pro football history.

The New York Giants were beating the Baltimore Colts, 17–14, with only 1:56 left to play. The Colts had the ball on their own 14-yard line as the Giants' defense dug in, determined to hold onto their slim lead and equally determined to walk off the field as NFL champions.

Baltimore quarterback, Johnny Unitas, spoke to his teammates in the huddle. "Now we're going to find out what we're made of," he said.

Unless the clock were to be stopped, Unitas would have no more time to huddle. From then on in, he would have to call his plays at the line of scrimmage.

The Colts lined up and Unitas went to work. Ever cool, and moving in an almost-unconscious, methodical fashion, Unitas hit Lenny Moore for an 11-yard gain. Then he threw to Raymond Berry for a 25-yard gain, to midfield. Again Unitas called on Berry, hitting him at the Giants' 35-yard line for a 15-yard gain. Realizing that he had a good thing going, Unitas reared back and again fired to Berry, this time for a 22-yard gain to the Giants' 13-yard line. With time running out, the Colts went to their field-goal specialist,

Steve Myhra, who booted a 20-yarder to send the game into overtime.

The Giants' fans were stunned. Now everything seemed to be going the Colts' way. In the overtime the Giants were stalled and forced to punt. The team that scored first would win the championship, and the Giants had given Unitas and his brilliant receivers another chance.

The Colts started on their own 20-yard line and soon they were on the Giants' 8. Within striking distance, the situation dictated caution. Surely Unitas would keep the ball on the ground. If he were to throw, the Giants' secondary might intercept and regain control of the game.

But Unitas threw caution and tradition to the wind by calling a daring play—a sideline pass to tight end Jim Mutscheller, who caught it at the 1-yard line. On the next play Unitas handed off to fullback Alan Ameche, who smashed through the Giants' line and scored. The Colts were victors, 23–17.

After the game Unitas was asked if he hadn't taken a high risk by passing to Mutscheller when an interception might have wrecked the Colts' chances.

His cool reply exemplified the kind of game he had just played. "When you know what you're doing," he said with a smile, "you don't get intercepted. I knew the play would work."

On average, more than 58,000 people
pay to attend each regular-season
National Football League game. In 1979 the
NFL recorded a total of 13,182,039 paid
admissions among the 28 teams during
the regular season. When did the attendance
mark first top the ten-million plateau?

In 1971 the NFL announced that 10,076,035
fans paid to see its teams in action.

Who said, "Once one has tasted the success
of being the very best it's hard to settle
for anything less"?

The one and only O. J. Simpson—who
should know about success, being the only man
to run for over 2,000 yards in one season.

When did San Diego Charger quarterback
Dan Fouts regret turning down
a post-game interviewer?

At the conclusion of the 1980 Oakland
Raider-San Diego Charger American Football
Conference championship game, Fouts was in
no mood for interviews. In fact when a reporter
approached him and thrust out a microphone,
Fouts growled "Get the --- microphone out of
my face."

Fouts seemed perturbed, but when he looked up he broke into a smile. "When you have to tell your father to get the mike out of your face, it's really bad," he said.

The quarterback's father, Bob Fouts, is a broadcaster for ABC in San Francisco, where Dan grew up, and formerly was the play-by-play man on the San Francisco 49ers broadcasts.

What is the difference between the I and Stacked I formations?

The I formation has the quarterback, half-back, and fullback in a straight line behind the center.

The stacked I adds the tight end to the line.

What were the lowest and highest game totals O. J. Simpson accumulated during his record-breaking 2,003-yard season in 1973?

O. J. Simpson managed only 55 yards on the ground in 14 tries in the season's sixth game, against the Miami Dolphins. Simpson's highest single-game total was 250 yards on 29 carries in the Bills' season opener at the expense of the New England Patriots.

Name the former Miami Dolphin
who observed, "All men are created equal . . .
except the great ones!"

Number 39 himself, Larry Csonka.

A member of the Houston Oilers
ran back interceptions on two consecutive plays.
Who was he?

Ken Houston, on December 19, 1971.

Who was the first defensive lineman
ever to be named Player of the Year by the
Football Writers of America?

Alan Page of the Minnesota Vikings won
the award in 1971.

Name the winner of the first World
Football League championship.

The Birmingham Americans beat the
Florida Blazers, 22–21, in 1974. It was a game
that produced little action until the fourth
quarter, when the Blazers scored all of their
points.

**In which championship game
did officials ask a team
to stop kicking the extra point?**

It was the 1940 National Football League title match between the Chicago Bears and the Washington Redskins. As the game's end approached, the Bears were asked to stop kicking extra points because officials were running low on their supply of footballs. The Bears were winning by such a large margin that they were asked to run or pass for the extra points. The final score was Chicago 73, Washington 0.

**Who was one of the first Olympic stars
to turn to professional football?**

In 1912, Jim Thorpe, one of the greatest athletes of all time, won the decathlon and pentathlon events for the United States Olympic team. However, Thorpe was compelled to return the medals because before the games he had inadvertently lost his amateur standing by playing semiprofessional baseball for $25 a week. The Olympic rules state that only amateurs can compete in the Games.

Jim turned to pro football in 1915, when he was offered $250 a week to play for the Canton Bulldogs. At the time, most players were being paid $50 a week—including Jim's teammate, the famous "win one for the Gipper," Knute Rockne.

Although his Olympic medals were taken from Thorpe, in 1950 he was voted best athlete of the 20th century by American sportswriters.

One of the strangest plays in football history took place when a player leaped off the bench to tackle an opponent. Who was that player and when did he execute his memorable tackle?

The 1954 Cotton Bowl game featured Rice against Alabama. At one point in the game, Dick Moegle, Rice's Most Valuable Player, broke into the clear and appeared en route to a 95-yard touchdown run. But Alabama's Tommy Lewis, after seeing his team unsuccessfully try to tackle Moegle, got off the bench and brought down the Rice ace. The referees awarded Rice a touchdown on the play, since both coaches agreed to that decision. The game ended with Rice winning 28–6 and Lewis apologizing to Moegle for his impetuous act.

Name the first-rate quarterback who once tried out for the St. Louis Cardinals baseball team.

Sammy Baugh, one of the top passers in professional football (he attempted 2,992 passes and completed 1,709 for a total of 22,085 yards and 186 touchdowns), helped the Washington

Redskins win five divisional titles and two championships. Yet when Baugh tried out for the 1938 St. Louis Cardinals, he couldn't make the team and was told to concentrate on football. He did.

Who comprised the Buffalo Bills' awesome offensive line in 1973, during O. J. Simpson's 2,003-yard rushing season?

Center Bruce Jarvis, guards Reggie McKenzie and Joe DeLamielleure, and tackles Dave Foley and Donnie Green were members of the offensive line that O. J. himself nicknamed the "Electric Company."

When did surgery for torn knee ligaments lead to the death of a promising young professional football player?

On December 14, 1965 Mack Lee Hill, a second-year fullback with the Kansas City Chiefs, died following surgery for the repair of torn knee ligaments. The 25-year-old player, nicknamed Mack the Truck, went into convulsions after surgery. The cause of his death, according to a team spokesman, was a "sudden and massive embolism of the blood clot after surgery."

Doctors who treated Hill reported that his

knee condition was rare and that there was no known treatment for it.

**A professional football game
once was moved from one city to another
because of discrimination charges.
Do you know why it happened?**

In January 1965, the American Football League All-Star Game was transferred from New Orleans to Houston after black players had complained of discrimination in the Louisiana city. The 21 blacks who were scheduled to play in the game voted to pack their bags because some were refused taxicab service and admittance to certain nightclubs. League officials were supportive of the decision.

**Which team holds the
National Football League record for
consecutive divisional championships?**

From 1950 through 1955, the Cleveland Browns won six straight divisional championships under the leadership of Paul Brown. In more recent years, Brown developed the Cincinnati Bengals into an NFL contender.

The New York Giants spent 31 years
in the Polo Grounds before moving
to their new home in Yankee Stadium.
When did they move and which team
did they play in their first home game?

The year was 1956. The first home game
at the Stadium drew 50,000 fans. The Giants
defeated the Pittsburgh Steelers, 38–10.

The New York Giants were one of the
cornerstones of the National Football League.
When were the Giants organized and
who was their first coach?

The year was 1925 and the head coach was
Robert Folwell. The New Yorkers finished their
inaugural year with a respectable record of eight
wins and four losses, placing them fourth in the
league standings.

**In 1965, during the feverish war
between the National Football League and
the American Football League, the
New York Jets signed two well-known
college quarterbacks to huge contracts.
Joe Namath was one. Who was the other?**

Exactly seven days after rewarding Joe Namath with the richest contract ever given a rookie in professional football, the Jets signed 1964 Heisman Trophy winner and Notre Dame graduate John Huarte. Huarte's contract was reported at $200,000 a year, considerably more than the Jets shelled out for Namath.

**During the 1960s Lance Alworth
established himself as one of pro football's
peerless wide receivers. During that time
he set two receiving records.
Why was this success so surprising,
and what were the two records Alworth set?**

Because of his blend of speed, timing, and balance, Lance Alworth was regarded by many critics as the finest receiver in either the American Football League or the National Football League. Between 1963 and 1968, he gained more than 1,000 yards in each of six straight seasons— a pro football record. In the last game of 1969 he added yet another amazing accomplishment. That game marked the 96th in a row in which Alworth had caught a pass; this broke the record of 95 games, set 24 years earlier by the legendary Don Hutson.

Alworth's success was surprising in view of the fact that his career got off on the wrong foot during his 1962 rookie season. Alworth injured his right thigh early in the season and was hobbled by it all year. As the pain in his leg increased, so did the accusations by his teammates that he was faking the injury. Some even suggested that he was fearful of pro football's rough play. Following the 1962 season it was determined that Alworth had not merely pulled the muscle but had torn it. Surgery was performed to repair the damage and Alworth rebounded from the injury to prove what a healthy Lance Alworth could accomplish on a football field.

Name the three Miami Dolphin stars who jumped to the now-defunct World Football League in 1975, after enjoying a Super Bowl-winning season in 1974.

Wide receiver Paul Warfield and running backs Larry Csonka and Jim Kiick switched to the World Football League's Memphis Southmen and provided the WFL with instant credibility. However, the WFL never found prosperity and folded a year and a half after its birth.

Steve Owen was the New York Giants'
most successful coach, leading them to
two National Football League championships.
How many years was Owen head coach
and who was his successor?

After starring on the Giants' offensive line, Owen was named head coach in 1931 and led the Polo Grounds–based club through 23 seasons, finally leaving New York at the completion of the 1953 campaign. Owen was replaced by Jim Lee Howell, who piloted the club for seven seasons.

Gale Sayers broke in with the Chicago Bears
in 1965 after an illustrious college career.
However, Sayers did not win
a starting berth immediately. How many games
passed before Sayers made it
to the Bears' varsity?

It wasn't until the fourth game of the 1965 season that Sayers got to start. Sayers scored once in his first starting role, four times in his second, and, late in the season, scored a record-tying six touchdowns in one game.

**Who holds the record
for most consecutive passes attempted
without having any intercepted?**

The Green Bay Packers' Bart Starr completed 294 passes without interception between 1964 and 1965.

Name the football coach who played right field for the New York Yankees before Babe Ruth.

George "Papa Bear" Halas was a switch-hitting prospect with the Bronx Bombers until an injury significantly reduced his speed and effectiveness as a player. Playing for the Yankees on an exhibition tour against the Brooklyn Dodgers, Halas attempted to stretch a double into a triple, tearing ligaments in the process. When Halas returned, he managed only two singles in 22 at bats. The Yankees demoted him to the minors soon after the 1919 season started. A year later the Yanks acquired Ruth, who more than amply filled in for Halas.

**Name the baseball manager who is believed
to have been the first quarterback
to use the T-formation.**

Charlie Dressen played on a team operated
by an Illinois businessman named A. E. Staley.
Dressen helped the Staleys' to a Central Illinois
title. Dressen went on to play professional baseball and to manage five different big-league
teams, including the Brooklyn Dodgers.

**In 1977 the National Football League's
entrance fee was $16,000,000. What was the fee
for joining the American Professional
Football Association in 1920?**

Each of the 11 APFA members put up $100
for what George Halas claimed was "the privi-
lege of losing money."

**Why was the name "American Professional
Football Association" somewhat pretentious?**

Because the 11 members represented only
four states—Ohio, New York, Michigan and
Illinois.

**Who were the Columbus Panhandles,
the Rochester Jeffersons, and the
Rock Island Independents?**

They were among the 11 charter members of the American Professional Football Association.

**This player also was president of the league
in which his team played. Who was he?**

Jim Thorpe could run, kick, and orchestrate a league. While president of the American Professional Football Association, Thorpe directed the Canton Bulldogs to the league's championship play-off. In the first round Canton was beaten by Buffalo, 7–3.

**Who holds the National Football League
record for the most field goals
in a regular season contest?**

Jim Bakken, placekicker for the St. Louis Cardinals, holds the record with seven field goals. Bakken accomplished the feat against the Pittsburgh Steelers on September 24, 1967, breaking Garo Yepremian's record of six.

Yepremian, who played for the Detroit Lions, had set the record of six in 1966 during a 32–31 Lion victory over the Minnesota Vikings.

131

Terry Bradshaw led the Pittsburgh Steelers
to three Super Bowl titles and
is regarded as one of the finest
contemporary quarterbacks. However,
he has suffered more than his share
of bad games. In 1975, Bradshaw experienced
what he considers the low point of his career.
What happened?

When Bradshaw came to the Steelers from
Louisiana Tech he was a mediocre passer lack-
ing consistency. In 1975, head coach Chuck Noll
benched Bradshaw in favor of Joe Gilliam. Bradshaw summed up his feelings thusly: "There was
bitterness [against Noll]. There was a lack of
communication. He didn't know how to talk to
me. There was animosity and bitterness, but
that's only natural when you feel you should be
playing."

Bradshaw regained his first-string spot and
eventually asserted himself as the leader the
Steelers so badly needed.

**When the Kansas City Chiefs
won the Super Bowl in 1970, their defense
received as much acclaim as the offense.
Name the Chiefs' linebackers on the
1970 championship team.**

The Kansas City linebackers included Willie Lanier in the middle and Bobby Bell and Jim Lynch on the outside. Lanier was one of the greatest middle linebackers in pro football.

**Before they were renamed the
New York Jets, the club's name was the Titans.
Name the last two original Titans
to have played for the Jets.**

Larry Grantham and Don Maynard.

The Titans were born in 1960 under the aegis of sportsman Harry Wismer. From day one the Titans were financially strapped. Grantham once said that in the three years during which Wismer owned the team, the gridders never even had a playbook. But in 1963, Wismer sold out and a new group of owners took over, renaming the team the Jets.

Maynard was one of the best of the original Titans, a superior pass-catcher. Grantham starred at linebacker for many years; even though he was neither big nor fast, he compensated with intelligence and determination.

What changes did the National Football League make in April 1974 to liven up the game?

Promising to make football livelier, the NFL instituted a 15-minute sudden-death overtime period to settle ties; moved the goal posts ten yards deeper into the end zone; and ruled that after a missed field goal the ball would be placed on the line of scrimmage or at the 20-yard line, whichever was farther from the goal line.

Changes adopted to protect wide receivers from the downfield battering they had been exposed to included a penalty reduction from 15 yards to 10 yards for offensive holding, tripping, and illegal use of hands. Also, the dangerous "crackback" blocks that had caused many injuries were banned.

The alterations were the most widespread the league had made since 1933, the year the goal posts were moved from the back of the end zone to the goal line to encourage field-goal kicking.

Can you recall the last National Football League team to survive an entire season undefeated and identify its backfield?

The Miami Dolphins went through the 1972 season unbeaten and untied, winning a total of 17 games. They won the Super Bowl against Washington, 14–7. The starting quarterback that year was Bob Griese; his backup was Earl Morrall. The starting backs were the NFL's version of Butch Cassidy and the Sundance Kid, otherwise known as Larry Csonka and Jim Kiick. The third back, Mercury Morris, rushed for 1,000 yards. Although Morris wasn't an extremely big man compared with other pro football players, he was capable of bench-pressing more weight than any of his teammates.

Who was the first black football player to lead his team in a Rose Bowl classic?

The first black to play in the Rose Bowl was Fritz Polland of Brown University in 1916. The first black quarterback was Sandy Stephens of Minnesota in 1961. But Charles West of Washington and Jefferson became the first black to lead a team when he played in the 1922 Rose Bowl. West was a halfback technically, but he "quarterbacked" his team because he called most of the plays for the squad.

In 1980, four members were elected into the Professional Football Hall of Fame. Who were they?

The 1980 selectees were Herb Adderley, who played most of his career with the Green Bay Packers; David "Deacon" Jones, the great defensive end for the Los Angeles Rams; Bob

Lilly of the Dallas Cowboys; and Jim Otto of the Oakland Raiders.

The charter class of 17 enshrinees was elected in 1963.

Has any team failed to score in a Super Bowl contest?

No—although some teams have come close.

In the biggest upset of Super Bowl history, on January 12, 1969, the New York Jets held the Baltimore Colts to one touchdown, in the fourth quarter. The Jets won, 16–7, in Super Bowl III.

Kansas City allowed only a four-yard touchdown run by Minnesota's running back Dave Osborn on January 11, 1970. This was Minnesota's only score as Kansas City went on to win Super Bowl IV, 23–7.

In 1972's Super Bowl VI, the Miami Dolphins lost to the Dallas Cowboys, 24–3. The Dolphins only score came as a result of Garo Yepremian's 31-yard field goal.

Washington managed to score their only touchdown with 7:07 left in the game in Super Bowl VII, on January 14, 1973. The Redskins lost to the Miami Dolphins, 14–7, in the lowest-scoring Super Bowl contest. Miami's win capped a perfect season. They already had won the previous 16 games they had played.

In Super Bowl VIII, played on January 13, 1974, Miami won again. This time the Dolphins held Minnesota to one touchdown, which came on a Fran Tarkenton scramble run from the 4-yard line. Miami ended the contest ahead, 24–7.

Minnesota came back the following year and again was held to one score, this time by the Pittsburgh Steelers. The Viking's Matt Blair blocked Bobby Walden's punt and Terry Brown recovered the ball in the end zone for a touchdown on January 12, 1975. The Steelers went on to win Super Bowl IX, 16–6.

In three Super Bowls, Minnesota scored a total of 20 points. Each score came on an irregular play. In their last Super Bowl appearance, the Vikings managed two scores against Oakland—one on a pass by Tarkenton and another via an aerial by Bob Lee.

Name the only father-son combination to have entries next to their names in the National Football League record book!

Dad scored a record six touchdowns against the Chicago Bears in 1951 and Junior completed 17 consecutive passes against the New York Jets in 1974. Dad, who played for the Cleveland Browns, is Dub Jones; and Junior is Bert Jones, star of the Baltimore Colts.

During the 1941 season
two National Football League teams
swapped cities. One of the owners at that time
still presides over his franchise. What were
the teams and who is the owner?

In 1941 the Philadelphia Eagles, owned by
Bert Bell and Art Rooney, moved to Pittsburgh,
while the Pittsburgh Steelers, owned by Alexis
Thompson, moved to Philadelphia. Rooney and
Bell assumed leadership of the Steelers, and
Thompson gained control of the Eagles. Rooney
is the current owner of the Steelers.

On January 29, 1959, a former
New York Giants offensive coach was signed
to a five-year pact as coach and general manager
of another National Football League franchise.
He then established what many believe
was the greatest dynasty in pro football.
Who was he and what did his teams accomplish?

Vince Lombardi became head coach of the
Green Bay Packers on January 29, 1959, and led
the Pack to five NFL titles between 1962 and
1967.

**In what year was a National Football League
title decided when a star player scored
the winning points for the opposing team?**

In the 1945 championship game between
the Cleveland Rams and the Washington Redskins, Sammy Baugh, the Washington quarterback, threw a pass from his own end zone that
was blown by the wind into the goal post. Under
the rules at that time, a safety was awarded to
the Rams. That made the score 2–0 Cleveland.
The Redskins managed two more touchdowns
but the Rams also scored twice (though missing
an extra point), making the final score Rams 15,
Redskins 14.

**At the conclusion of the 1980 season,
he was the second-winningest coach in
college football history. Who is this coaching
legend, and who is the only man with
more victories?**

Alabama's Paul "Bear" Bryant has won 306
games, lost 80, and tied 16 in 35 years. Bryant's
success places him only eight victories shy of
Amos Alonzo Stagg's record of 314 wins.

Two National Football League coaches
active in the 1980 season were once
the leading pass receivers in the NCAA.
Who are they, and in what years did they lead
the college ranks in receiving?

Neil Armstrong, head coach of the Chicago Bears, caught 39 passes for 317 yards in 1943 while playing for Oklahoma A&M (now Oklahoma State). Jim Hanifan, head coach of the St. Louis Cardinals, led all college receivers in 1954 with 44 catches for 569 yards, while playing for the University of California.

Not all National Football League aces
launched their careers as stars. This quarterback
was a 17th-round draft pick in 1956 and
rode the bench for three seasons behind
such noted passers as Tobin Rote, Babe Parilli,
Joe Francis, and Lamar McHan. Eventually
he led his team to five NFL championships.
He later coached the team he once
quarterbacked. Who was this
late-blossoming star?

Bart Starr came out of the University of Alabama and then rode the bench while the Packers suffered successive 4–8, 3–9, and 1–10–1 seasons. With the arrival of Vince Lombardi in 1959, Starr was relegated to third-string quarterback. However, late in the season, McHan was injured and Lombardi was not satisfied with

Francis. Starr got his chance, and he led Green Bay to four consecutive victories. The following season (1960), Starr led the Packers to the Western Division title.

This passing legend closed out his career by using his powerful right arm for something other than throwing a football. Who was he, and what made the final game of his illustrious career so notable?

Sammy Baugh took the field for the Washington Redskins on opening day, 1952. It marked the last time he would quarterback the Redskins during his 16-year career. Baugh, who was not at full strength because of a preseason hand injury, was taunted throughout the game by Chicago Cardinals tackle Don Joyce. Finally, after Joyce sacked him, Baugh cocked his right arm and aimed it at Joyce's head. The fight resulted in the ejection of both players. Baugh never returned to quarterback the Redskins.

One of the lesser-known upsets in pro football championship play occurred on December 19, 1935, when the Detroit Lions won the National Football League title from the defending champs. Whom did the Lions defeat?

The Detroit Lions were the surprise of the pro football world in the 1935 season. After an early-season record of 3–3–2, they suddenly rebounded, winning four straight games and beating out heavily favored Green Bay for the Western Division title. Few took the Lions seriously when they faced the mighty New York Giants—rated the most powerful team in all football—for the NFL title.

But Lions head coach George "Potsy" Clark had other ideas. New York was renowned for its passing game, so Clark set out to nullify it. He devised plans to keep the Giants on the ground, knowing that the Detroit line was fast and could contain the Giants' running game.

Clark's strategy proved to be successful, as Detroit triumphed, 26–7. The game was played on a snow- and rain-soaked field, which worked in favor of the Lions. New York could never establish its passing or running superiority, and the Lions wasted no time exploiting the Giants' misfortune.

As 15,000 fans at Detroit Stadium looked on, the Lions attacked first. Glen Presnell passed to Ed Klewicki to move the Lions into scoring position. From there, Ace Gutowsky scored on a two-yard run. The extra point was good, giving the Lions a 7–0 lead. Detroit scored again when Dutch Clark ran 42 yards to paydirt. After a scoreless second quarter, the Lions went into halftime with a 13–0 lead.

In the second half, the Giants scored when Ed Danowski completed a 42-yard touchdown toss to Ken Strong. It proved to be the Giants' lone touchdown. The Lions persisted. They scored again on a run by Ernie Caddel and completed the romp with a final drive that was capped by a nine-yard dash by Buddy Parker. They left the Giants in shambles to become the 1935 NFL champs.

At the start of the 1969 season, New York Jets quarterback Joe Namath was suspended by the National Football League for reasons unrelated to action on the girdiron. Why was Namath temporarily banished?

"Broadway" Joe Namath owned an interest in a Manhattan bar called Bachelors III. Supposedly, he had been told that the bar had been a meeting place for bookmakers, narcotics dealers, hired gunmen, and top-ranking Mafia officials. NFL officials notified Namath to sell his share of the bar or he would be banned from pro football. It was also reported that bets on football games were being placed from telephones in the bar. At first Namath resisted the NFL ultimatum and "retired" from football. But he soon relented and sold his interest in Bachelors III.

**This football luminary is second
on the all-time total-points list, led the league
in field goals five times, and scored
in 107 consecutive games. He also had
a very appropriate nickname. Who was he?**

Lou "The Toe" Groza, amassed 1,349 points in his 17 seasons, all with the Cleveland Browns. He is second only to George Blanda on the all-time points list. Groza led the NFL in field goals in 1950, 1952, 1953, 1954, and 1957, and between 1950 and 1959 scored in 107 consecutive games.

**The National Football League
championship games began in 1933. However,
eight years later a mere 13,341 fans attended
the title match between the Chicago Bears
and the New York Giants. What was the reason
for such poor attendance?**

The game was held on December 21, 1941; just two weeks earlier, the Japanese had bombed Pearl Harbor. Americans evidently had war on their minds, not football.

This receiver could hardly see without glasses,
his right leg was a quarter-inch shorter
than his left, and he had chronic back problems.
Yet he led the National Football League
in receptions three times. Who was this stellar,
if troubled, pass catcher?

Raymond Berry spent 12 seasons with the
Baltimore Colts. He led the NFL in receptions in
1958, 1959, and 1960. He is third on the all-time
receiving list, with 631 catches. Only Don Maynard (633) and Charley Taylor (635) have
more. Berry was inducted into the Hall of Fame
in 1973.

The first black player the Giants ever signed
was a star defensive back who went on to
become the first full-time black coach
in pro football. Name this NFL pioneer.

Emlen Tunnell starred for ten years with
the Giants, gaining 1,282 yards, all on defense.
He intercepted 79 passes during his career,
second on the all-time list. Tunnell finished his
career with the Green Bay Packers and went on
to become the assistant defensive coach of the
Giants.

On November 8, 1970, a professional
football record was set by a man who,
because of a birth defect, had half a foot
and no right hand. Who was he
and what was the record?

On the last play of the game between the
Detroit Lions and the New Orleans Saints, Tom
Dempsey, the Saints' 23-year-old placekicker,
was called on to attempt a 63-yard field goal.
The attempt was good. Dempsey set a new field-
goal record (breaking Baltimore Colt Bert
Rechichar's mark by seven yards), and the
Saints won the game, 19–17. Dempsey later said
that because he was too far away, he never saw
the ball clear the crossbar.

During the 1972–73 season, the Miami Dolphins
went undefeated through the 14-game
regular season as well as a 14–7 Super Bowl
victory over the Washington Redskins.
The Dolphins might have won the Super Bowl
game by a score of 14–0, were it not
for a most unusual play by a Miami player.
What was the play?

With two minutes and seven seconds left in
the game, Dolphin placekicker Garo Yepremian
attempted to pass a blocked 42-yard field goal

attempt. Pass it he did—right into the hands of Redskin cornerback Mike Bass, who scampered 49 yards for the score. Yepremian had a chance to stop Bass, but the 155-pounder missed the tackle.

He played for the Pittsburgh Pirates and the Detroit Lions between 1938 and 1941, leading the league in rushing in 1938 and 1940, and then went on to become an associate justice of the Supreme Court. Who was he?

Byron "Whizzer" White rushed for 567 yards in 1938 and 514 yards in 1940, leading the league both times. In 1962 he was appointed to the United States highest court by President John F. Kennedy.

This running star had two problems early on in his career. First, at 188 pounds, he was small for a running back. Second, he had to fill the shoes of one of the NFL's most accomplished runners. Who was he and whom did he replace?

During rookie camp in May 1964, Leroy Kelly was told by Cleveland Browns coach Blanton Collier, "I wish you were bigger." Kelly returned to camp in July weighing 200 pounds. Two years later, Kelly replaced the legendary

Jim Brown. In 1967 and 1968, Kelly led the NFL in rushing. He finished his career in 1973, having rushed for 7,274 yards.

On December 16, 1973, on a snowy Shea Stadium field, a rushing record was set and a distinguished coaching career ended. What was the record, who set it, and who was the coach who directed his last game?

O. J. Simpson, playing for the Buffalo Bills, established a single-season rushing mark while leading the Bills to a 34–14 victory over the New York Jets. The loss marked the final game in the 20-year career of Jets coach Weeb Ewbank.

On December 12, 1965, Chicago Bears running back Gale Sayers tied a record that had been set 36 years earlier and had been matched only once in the intervening years. What was that record?

Sayers scored six touchdowns as the Bears beat the San Francisco 49ers, 61–20. Ernie Nevers, playing for the Chicago Cardinals, scored six touchdowns and added four points-after-touchdown, a total of 40 points, on November 28, 1929; and Dub Jones scored six times for the Cleveland Browns on November 25, 1951.

In the introduction to this legendary
running back's autobiography, comedian
Bill Cosby wrote, "I saw [him] split.
He just split in two.
He threw the right side of his body one way
and the left side of his body kept going.
The defensive men didn't know who to catch."
To whom was Cosby referring?

In Gale Sayers's autobiography, *I Am Third*,
Cosby recalls watching Sayers make that remarkable move during a Pro Bowl game in Los
Angeles. Ram tackle Rosey Grier attempted to
tackle Sayers. As the 300-pound Grier recalls,
"I hit him so hard, I thought my shoulder must
have busted him in half. I heard the crowd roar,
so I figured he must have fumbled. I started
scrambling around, looking for the loose ball.
But there was no loose ball, and Sayers was
gone." Sayers had sped 80 yards for a touchdown.

New York Giants coach Steve Owen
once commented that there was "only one
defense that could stop [him]—shoot him
before he leaves the dressing room."
About whom was Owen talking?

Owen was referring to Chicago Bears fullback Bronko Nagurski. Nagurski played both
fullback and tackle for the Bears between 1930
and 1937; the Giants and Bears met for the

National Football League championship twice during that time, each team winning once.

Before the start of the 1955 season, the Pittsburgh Steelers made what eventually became a terrible mistake. What was that mistake?

During training camp the Steelers cut a young quarterback by the name of John Unitas. Unitas spent the 1955 season playing for a Pittsburgh semipro team. In 1956 he joined the Baltimore Colts, and in 1958 he led them to the National Football League championship. He went on to become one of the game's foremost quarterbacks.

On November 18, 1968, the National Broadcasting Company committed a programming blunder that outraged football fans. What error did NBC make, and what circumstances followed the foul-up?

At precisely 7:00 P.M., NBC stopped televising the New York Jets–Oakland Raiders game with one minute left to play in the game and the outcome still undecided, and switched to network programming of the movie *Heidi*. The NBC switchboard was so flooded with calls that eventually it broke down. The Raiders went on to score two touchdowns in the final minute and win the game, 43–32.

When, and for what purpose, was sudden-death overtime first used by the National Football League?

In November 1940, the NFL announced that sudden death would be used to decide tie games between teams that were deadlocked for the division lead at the end of the regular season. At that time the NFL consisted of two divisions, East and West.

"A streak of fire, a breath of flame;
    Eluding all who reach and clutch;
A gray ghost thrown into the game
That rival hands may rarely touch."
Who wrote these words, and about whom was he writing?

Sportswriter Grantland Rice was describing Illinois University running back Red Grange. In three years of varsity football at Illinois, Grange ran for 31 touchdowns in 20 games and amassed 3,637 yards rushing and returning punts and kickoffs.

**During the 1930s this gifted black man
was playing football for the
University of California at Los Angeles,
but he was to make his mark in a different sport.
Who was he?**

In the spring of 1947, Jackie Robinson was signed by Branch Rickey, general manager of the Brooklyn Dodgers, thereby becoming the first black to play major league baseball. Robinson starred in the UCLA backfield during his college career.

**Who was the first man ever
to break the 10,000-yard rushing mark?
How many players have accomplished the feat?**

Jim Brown was the first player to rush for more than 10,000 yards in a pro career. On November 1, 1964, Brown gained 149 yards in a game against the Pittsburgh Steelers, to bring his career total to 10,135 yards. By the time he left the game in 1965, Brown had rushed for a total of 12,312 yards. As of 1980, O. J. Simpson is the only other player to break the 10,000-yard barrier.

He was an All-American in basketball and
football at Northwestern University.
He played four musical instruments.
He was not accepted as a top-notch quarterback,
however, until he led his team to
three National Football League titles.
Who was this passing great?

Otto Graham led the Cleveland Browns to
four All-America Football Conference championships before the Browns joined the NFL in
1950. He then led Cleveland to six division titles
in six years, including three NFL championships.
He eventually became head coach of the Washington Redskins.

Before a 1924 game between his unbeaten
University of Michigan team and the
University of Illinois, coach Fielding Yost
declared that a certain Illinois player would be
"Carefully watched every time he takes the ball.
There will be 11 clean, hard Michigan tacklers
headed for him." Those 11 tacklers had
a hard time catching up with that
Illinois running back, who threw or ran
for all six of Illinois' touchdowns as
the Illini downed Michigan, 39–14. He went on
to star with the Chicago Bears
of the NFL. Who was he?

Red "The Galloping Ghost" Grange, despite his relatively small (6'0", 170-pound) frame, was a three-time All-American at Illinois. He played his rookie season with the Bears and then moved on to the New York Yankees of the American Football League, which he helped organize. He returned to the Bears until injuries forced him to retire in 1935.

Since the award's inception in 1935, how many strictly defensive players have won the Heisman Trophy?

None.
Of the 46 winners to date, only two players who played defense have won the award. However, both Larry Kelly of Yale (1936) and Leon Hart of Notre Dame (1949) played both offense and defense. The award has gone to either a running back or a quarterback every other year.

This football great, who never made it to the pros, once declared, "Football isn't my game." Who said this?

George Gipp, a Notre Dame football star, informed coach Knute Rockne that he was not interested in playing football. Gipp originally had come to Notre Dame on a baseball and basketball scholarship, but Rockne persuaded him to play football. After an illustrious career with Notre Dame, he was drafted by the Chicago White Sox. He was named to the college football All-American team, but never played professionally. After the 1919 season, Gipp died of pneumonia.

Name the former Washington Redskins coach who is believed to have been the author of the saying "Winning isn't everything; it's the only thing."

Most football fans will be quick to name Vince Lombardi but, according to the Washington Star's Morris Siegal, the answer is Joe Kurharich. In an article written by Dave Anderson of the *New York Times*, Siegal revealed that a search through the clips of his newspaper showed that Kurharich first uttered those now famous lines at a Redskins' welcome-home luncheon in 1954, long before Lombardi became nationally known as the originator of what has turned out to be one of professional sports' most popular credos.

Probably because during his nine-year

coaching career he coached only two winners (The 1955 Redskins were 8–4 and the 1966 Philadelphia Eagles were 9–5) Kurharich never became known as one of sport's true artists of the spoken word. However, as Anderson showed in a column which appeared on January 29, 1980, Kurharich could hold his own with Casey Stengal, Lombardi and other sportsmen who are as well known for their gift of gab as their athletic feats.

When Kurharich was with the Eagles, the team swapped their quarterback Sonny Jurgensen for the Washington Redskins' Q.B. Norm Snead. At the announcement of the deal Kurharich said: "Trading quarterbacks is a rarity, but it's not unusual." Another time Kurharich, always the astute observer, noted of a certain game that "We were three points behind, but that's not the same as being even." Some of his other more memorable remarks include, "I can only answer a question about a conclusive." "The charge on that blocked kick came either from the inside or the outside." "I'm not vacillating you." "Every coach must view a player with three different eyes."

Kurharich coached the Chicago Cardinals in 1952, the Redskins from 1954-1958 and the Eagles from 1964-1968. His lifetime record was 62-81-3. Kurharich is also the answer to another popular trivia question: Name the only coach to compile a losing record while at Notre Dame.

As a guard for the Fighting Irishmen, Kurharich from 1935-1937 was a member of the All-Midwest team of 1937, but he did not enjoy much success as a coach. Between 1959 and 1962 Notre Dame went 17-23. His most successful year as a college or pro coach came in 1951 when his University of San Francisco team went undefeated in nine games. Two players from that team, Ollie Matson and Gino Marchetti, went on to Pro Football's Hall of Fame.

The biggest battle of Kurharich's life took place off the football field. In 1970 doctors told him that he had bone cancer and would only live another 30 months. Taking as many as 36 pills a day and ignoring doctors orders to rest, Kurharich vowed that he wasn't going to let the disease get the best of him and continued, in his own way, to fight it. He continued to keep himself busy and in 1975 doctors found that his condition had improved enough for them to stop his chemotherapy treatments and he even began working again as an observer of National Football League Game officials. Two weeks before Super Bowl XV, in January of 1981, Kurharich's cancer returned and he had to be hospitalized. "I don't know what's going to happen," Dave Anderson quoted Kurharich as telling National Football League commissioner Pete Rozelle who had been Sports Information Director at the University of San Francisco when Kurharich coached there, "but I'm going to fight it." The night before Super Bowl XV, January 24, 1981, Kurharich died. The cancer had caught up with him, ten years after doctors had told him he had only 30 months to live.

FUN & GAMES FROM WARNER BOOKS

BAR GAMES BETS AND CHALLENGES
by Alan Ericksen (V90-648, $1.95)
Here are all the basic rules, preliminaries, descriptions of play, psychology of play and tips on barroom games using coins or paper money, matches, swizzle sticks, coasters, and even olives. Ericksen shows how to figure the probabilities and odds as well as do all the tricks.

THE AMAZIN' BILL MAZER'S BASEBALL TRIVIA BOOK
by Bill Mazer and Stan Fischler (S91-784, $2.50)
Bill Mazer is the sportscaster that nobody can beat. Now he makes you an expert too. The record makers and breakers; blasts from baseball's past; game anecdotes and player stories you won't want to miss; and little-known facts and figures. Bill Mazer has the facts and gives them to you in amusing anecdotes, quickie quizzes, and question and answer stumpers.

BARTENDER'S GUIDE TO BASEBALL
by Dick Lally (S91-736, $2.50)
Forty challenging quizzes containing over 2000 questions and answers, this book covers the whole range of baseball under short subject areas. Pitching, hitting, World Series, Hall of Fame, rookies, All Star Game MVP and even a section on baseball movies.

HIGH & INSIDE
The Complete Guide to Baseball Slang
by Joseph McBride (S91-939, $2.50)
This book answers the question "Why do they call it . . .?" for over 1000 baseball terms and nicknames. Loaded with definitions and origins plus a dictionary of nicknames with the background of each. And baseball one-liners that have been quoted often with their courses and stories.

GREAT SPORTS READING
FROM WARNER BOOKS

TIME ENOUGH TO WIN
by Roger Staubach & Frank Luksa   (S30-034, $2.95)
The #1 all-time NFL quarterback tells his own story. From his rivalry with Coach Landry over who should call the plays to his decision to retire—from the greatest game he ever played to the faith that guided him in his violent career—Staubach tells all.

THE YOUNG RUNNERS' HANDBOOK
by Elizabeth G. Barley & Mark Bloom   (S90-999, $1.95)
All the information anyone aged 7 to 14 needs to run. Includes stretching and strengthening exercises, information on equipment to buy, what to do about specific aches and pains, how to start a running program and a running club, games to play to make running more fun—and lots more.

To order, use the coupon below. If you prefer to use your own stationery, please include complete title as well as book number and price. Allow 4 weeks for delivery.